The Software Soul

Unleashing the spirit of software teams to maximize productivity

Mala Devlin

The Software Soul

ISBN: 978-0-578-03265-8

To learn more about The Software Soul and to join the discussion, visit www.TheSoftwareSoul.com

This book is dedicated to my family and friends,

in gratitude for

their support and encouragement.

_____

CONTENTS

Section 4: The Software Soul

Section 5: People Focused Operations

Section 6: Transformations

Appendices

PREFACE

I truly enjoy being a software engineering manager. I wrote this book to share best practices on how to create great engineering teams and maximize their productivity. After all, it is people that build software products. Happy engineering teams, which are set up for success, naturally create better products.

Over the last 20 years, I have worked in a number of software companies and in a variety of roles: first as a software developer, then as a product manager and subsequently as a software engineering manager. It has been my good fortune to work on some amazing teams in highly successful technology companies. The ability to build innovative products with best-in-class engineers is a great experience. Taking a project from inception through to delivery is always a roller coaster ride. Getting a good quality software product shipped is unbelievably difficult! I have the deepest respect for all engineering teams that can do this consistently.

I have also had my share of failures and been part of teams that were simply dysfunctional and unable to deliver even basic requirements. This diverse set of hands-on experiences has given me deep insight into what it takes to build good software products and software teams.

What makes software so unique? In a software system, there are hundreds of ways in which a problem can be solved – each with its set of tradeoffs. Having this great latitude is a mixed blessing. There are no sure fire paths to success. Software's malleability opens up a large number of options in solving problems. Teams that can iterate quickly through the maze of possibilities and adapt to new information are the ones that will succeed.

Unleashing productivity in engineering teams is critical to speeding up the iterative cycle. The speed of engineering iteration and problem solving makes the difference between an average team and one that can consistently deliver great products.

That is, *how a team feels and works together* makes all the difference.

I moved into engineering management because I wanted to have greater business impact. Setting up a team of smart engineers to succeed was something I saw as both challenging and critical for business success. During my formal management training I learned about project management and assessing technology risks and tradeoffs. Yet, at a practical level, this training did not prepare me adequately to face the challenges of managing engineering teams. I needed to adapt my management style from purely managing technology and projects to paying more attention to people and teams. People management took up most of my time. Initially, I was quite irritated because that was not my vision of what an engineering manager should do. I thought I would spend most of my time tinkering with cool technology. But this was not the case. In reality, I had to be good at setting up teams of smart engineers to succeed. I learned this the hard way. Although I consider myself a "people person", I found I had a lot to learn when I actually became an engineering manager.

Over the years, my love of technology was eclipsed by my love for growing great engineering teams. I have always been attracted to challenges. It became obvious to me that people and teams were much harder to shape than software. To create good software, you need good teams – so, I knew where I needed to focus my energies as an engineering manager. Unleashing the potential in teams is really what engineering management is all about. Once I learned that, it made a world of difference.

The idea to write a book grew out of discussions with my good friend and colleague Soumya Viswanathan. We shared many of the same observations. We decided to conduct a series of interviews through 2008 to gather a wide array of viewpoints on the subject. We interviewed about 60 people – engineers, managers, and executives from a variety of fortune 1000 software engineering companies in Silicon Valley. We were on a quest to find out why some engineering teams are successful while others are mediocre. This difference seemed to be a key ingredient for business success.

This book is the outcome of those discussions. There are many case studies and examples gleaned from our interviews, along with recommendations on how to rethink software operations and software teams. Some of the recommendations are unorthodox. Our intention is to spark a dialogue on the possibilities and pave the way for a healthier and happier framework for software engineering teams.

I hope you enjoy reading this book as much as I enjoyed writing it. It has indeed been a very rewarding experience, and it is my pleasure to share this with you.

INTRODUCTION

The statistics for software project success rates are humbling [1]. Consider the following: more than half of all software projects fail and never make it out the door; more than half the cool features and products never get used by end customers and fail to generate the promised sales; a significant proportion of software products require armies of support engineers and are considered difficult to use. These failures significantly impact the bottom line: profitability of the products suffers.

It is now more important than ever to fully leverage and optimize software development and delivery. Why? Software has become a very critical part of our global economy. Twenty five years ago, the pursuit of software was something exotic and only the brave and few ventured into that area. Today, software is ubiquitous. It has woven itself into the very fabric of our society – from how we communicate, to the gadgets we use to the vehicles we drive. In fact, it is a key underpinning of the modern Western lifestyle. Good, reliable and technologically advanced software has become critical to our lifestyles and our economy.

Why is developing and delivering good software so difficult?

Many processes, tools, and methodologies have been introduced over the years to improve software development and increase the likelihood of successful product delivery. These have all helped to *some* extent. However, it has become apparent that there is something much more fundamental that needs attention.

Many software teams are simply not effective. In the midst of the rush, chaos, and excitement of software development, the engineers and teams become secondary to the product. It has become accepted practice in many circles to tolerate bully management, pontificating prima donnas, and rude email exchanges. It is believed that a technically virile leader with some smart engineers is all that is needed to create a success story. But, that is not the reality. The reality is that teams of very smart people are often not able to work together at their full potential. Business results suffer. Software projects often fail because teams are not fully leveraged and set up for success.

If we could harness the full energy of all these people, they would be more productive and produce better software, and companies would benefit and make a lot more money. Things *could sizzle* with the right ingredients – but, how?

As we started to look at what influenced behavior in a professional environment, we found it was the untold rules and methods by which the organization ran. The culture! People use phrases like "this is how things are done here" and "our management expects this behavior." So we set down the path of understanding how a software company's management team could nurture the type of culture that would maximize the productivity of its engineering team. That is, how can a business tap into the very *soul* of the software engineer to unleash their maximum potential?

There seemed no better resource in understanding company culture than people. We talked to senior engineers, technical leaders, managers, directors, and CEOs. We wanted to hear from them directly about their experiences. What does success look like and how can a company create a culture to maximize the probability of success in software engineering? We looked across people's experiences for common themes and for stark differences. Each told us something about how people succeeded or failed in their attempts at collective achievement.

Bottom Line

The software industry is an extremely competitive environment. Success is more probable for those management teams that can effectively harness the tremendous brain power of engineering professionals. A great culture is an essential tool that enables the delivery of advanced, pioneering technology on time with high quality, strong customer satisfaction which in turn builds a loyal customer base and ultimately profit growth.

The secret sauce is tapping into the *software soul* of the engineering team, and unleashing their full potential. The art of enabling such a culture and harnessing the spirit of the engineering team is what this book is all about.

WHAT YOU WILL FIND IN THIS BOOK

The following is an outline of each of the major sections in this book. There is a brief summary of the section, along with the key questions addressed in that section.

Section 1: People

A Critical part of any Software Program

Although it is obvious that people shape business outcomes, this fact is often overlooked or viewed as an annoyance by many software managers. This section explores why that is the case through an example and illustrates how many software projects eventually turn into maintenance nightmares. The section concludes by illustrating a framework for software success.

Here are the key questions addressed:

- What makes software challenging?
- What are typical pitfalls in software development?
- Why are people and teams important?
- What is the framework for software success?

Section 2: Leaders

Seeds of Inspiration and Values

Inspirational leaders are a rarity in software engineering. Technical virility rules as the key attribute that is most sought after in engineering management. As a result, many of the basic management skills are scarce in the realm of engineering management. This section explores how the fundamentals of engineering management are more than just about technology and the mechanics of project management. A leader's people skills and the leadership ecosystem shape management success – and ultimately business success.

Here are the key questions addressed:

- How do engineering managers shape the success of teams and products?
- What are traits of good engineering managers?
- What is the role of sponsorship?
- How does one nurture collaborative teams?
- How does one build a strong leadership web?

Section 3: Community

The Cultural Epicenter

Traditional communities share a common culture shaped by history, geography, language and rituals. Even with this common fabric, we see that many traditional communities have to battle a myriad of problems to thrive and succeed as a cohesive unit. A software community is unique in that it is often virtual, geographically distributed, lacking in inspirational leaders and common rituals. As such, it is a miracle that any software team can actually succeed. In fact, many simply implode. This section explores the core pillars for building a strong "software village" and how these shape team productivity and business success.

Here are the key questions addressed:

- What cultural pillars enable strong, fun teams?
- How do roles and responsibilities shape teams?
- Do gadgets help or detract from effective communications?
- Do virtual, multi-site teams really work or is it a fad?
- What is the true cost of offshoring?

- How does diversity shape teams?
- What is team esteem and how does it influence team success?
- What are team rituals and how do they strengthen teams?

Section 4: The Software Soul

Enabling a Strong Heartbeat

Many of us have experienced being part of amazing teams. It is a great experience. There is a magic energy that drives the team to high levels of performance, and an internal compass that points the team in the right direction. Such a team requires very little management and can achieve very high levels of success. This section explores the key factors that fuel this magic energy and how this enables happier, more productive teams.

Here are the key questions addressed:

- How can the magic energy be unleashed?
- What is the internal compass that guides software teams?
- How can a team be *driven* to succeed – beyond metrics and milestones?
- What are the three core values that most engineers hold dear?
- What does take to win the "Engineering Olympics" of innovation?
- How does the reward and recognition framework impact productivity and how can it be more effective?
- How does PowerPoint engineering influence software culture?

Section 5: People-Focused Operations

Unleashing the Spirit

How does one enable a vibrant culture and optimize team productivity within the organization's operational framework? That is what people-focused operations is all about. It is beyond metrics and methodologies. This section introduces the role of a team effectiveness coach as a catalyst for creating a broader set of factors that need to be considered when making business decisions.

Here are the key questions addressed:

- What does culture have to do with engineering operations?
- What is the Engineering Triumvirate?
- What is the role of a team effectiveness coach?
- How does one enable a strong team pulse?

Section 6: Transformations

An Enlightened Path

It is all fine to read about new ideas, but how do we put them into practice? This section offers suggestions on how to transcend the product lifecycle, enable engineering productivity and tap into the very soul and roots of change.

Here are the key questions addressed:

- What are the key elements in harnessing the power of your engineering teams?
- What is the role of formal training and colleges in shaping software leaders?
- How will you move forward to transform your teams and fully unleash their power?

Intended Audience

This book is for engineering managers, program managers, executives and management consultants who want to gain greater insight into what it takes to build great software teams, and unleash their spirit to maximize productivity.

ABOUT THE STORIES IN THIS BOOK

The majority of stories in this book are based on sixty interviews conducted during 2008. These stories were gleaned by interviewing engineers, managers and executives across a variety of Fortune 1000 Silicon Valley tech companies. The names and details of the scenarios have been modified to protect the anonymity of the interviewee.

Each person shared many tales of successes and failures. Many of the interviewees spent time discussing how they overcame difficult situations in their career and how that shaped their careers. Their stories are thought-provoking. Many of these stories will strike a chord, spark a debate or spur you into action. They are meant to do all of that. By examining the lessons learned from these failures, we get valuable insight into how we can improve the software culture and build a framework for success.

I would like to cite a couple of books that have examined failures as a means to foster success.

'Success through Failure' by Henry Petroski [2] contains stories about engineering failures and how great engineering feats build on the lessons learned from previous failures. One line that caught my attention is: "How individuals react to failures separates leaders from followers, true designers from mere users of things".

That is, we can use the failures in these stories to help us a design a set of success factors and create more positive software culture. This is the lightning rod to take the lead in making a difference.

Another book is 'Five Dysfunctions of a Team' by Patrick Lencioni [3]. This book studies the dysfunction of an executive team and provides a framework for team success. To understand team success factors, the author examines the failures of a particular executive team and then develops a team success framework.

The stories in this book are fashioned in the same spirit: learning from failures to pave a path for success. They illustrate the common pitfalls one faces in software engineering, and how engineering managers can create a more people-focused environment to harness the full power of their software teams.

A quote from the American author Napoleon Hill captures this spirit "Most great people have attained their greatest success just one step beyond their greatest failure".

I hope you enjoy reading these stories and are able to learn from them to pave a better path for you and your software engineering teams.

People

A Critical Part of any Software Program

"Things which matter most must never be at the mercy of things which matter least" ... Goethe

ENGINEERS ARE PEOPLE TOO

There has been much discussion about improving the success rates of software projects. Much thought and discussion have resulted in software engineering methodologies, coding and design guidelines, testing techniques, process improvements, and productivity tools. All these provide great ideas on how software teams can improve predictability, quality and productivity. Many companies have also adopted a wide array of these techniques. In spite of this, there remains a high degree of uncertainty in the software product development lifecycle. With all the brain power and smart people that work in the software business, it surprises me that we still have such a high failure rate. Even though we are trying to follow all the well-known trusted software development rules, the industry is far from realizing its full potential. Something is missing – and it is hurting the bottom line.

What is the secret sauce? There must be another set of enablers that also impacts the outcome.

As with many things, we sometimes miss the obvious. And the obvious can indeed be the "secret sauce". Software products are created by smart, highly creative and talented software engineers. How these individuals think, feel, and work together makes a huge difference in the overall excellence of the resulting software product – and ultimately its profitability. Unleashing the spirit of software teams to bring out their best is an art. It is the secret sauce that makes all the difference – and it has a huge impact on your bottom line.

Think about it... a team that is highly motivated, and driven by passion can always be counted on to "do the right thing" – with little bureaucratic monitoring and intervention. It is as if they had an internal compass that guides them through the ups and downs of creating good software on time. That internal compass and passion fosters a "can do" attitude and energizes the team to overcome the inevitable obstacles along the way. Further, it reduces the need for bureaucracy and bean counting that often permeate many software organizations. Engineers can focus on creating rather than just doing. The spirit inspires the team to work together, make the right technical decisions, and create cool software faster. Now, isn't that what all companies want?

Methodology Mania *vs* Software Spirit

Many software organizations still operate solely under the old school "software factory" and have translated the product development lifecycle into a myriad of processes, metrics and gates to control and mold the software that is produced. I have never liked the term Software Factory. The very term sucks the life out of engineers. The picture it evokes is one of monotonous work done by low wage workers, who are watching the clock and waiting to go home.

Software engineers pride themselves on their creativity and their ability to take on any challenge. In fact, *real* engineers like to take on tough challenges and they are in a constant state of problem solving and invention. They don't just solve problems from 9-5; they love the challenge and are constantly looking for ways to solve a problem better, faster and more innovatively. The last thing any self respecting engineer wants to work on are tasks that are highly repeatable, easy or requires bureaucratic gymnastics to complete. These are certainly competing forces.

On the one hand, companies want the benefits of a factory that delivers high quality, predictable products. On the other hand, software engineers cannot be managed like factory workers. Software engineers are in fact more like artists. Their creativity and emotional spirit have a huge impact on the product outcome. So, how do you tap into the spirit of these software artists in a way that maximizes creativity, drive, productivity – and marry this gracefully with the predictability of the software development process? A successful pairing of these philosophies – predictability and creativity - can result in improvements in productivity, quality and innovation, resulting in *sustained* profitability.

It's really *Harderware*

The duality of what it takes to inspire and motivate the software soul needs to coexist with the predictability of the software development processes. In general, we have tended to focus more on process and bean counting, and spend little if any time on inspiring, leading and motivating software engineering teams.

We do that because it is easier to manage by looking at things we can see and measure. Intangibles such as emotions, pride, and motivation take more time and effort to monitor. It is simply easier to see whether all the code reviews were done rather than having a conversation with your teams about whether they are set up for success. The code review has a binary yes or no answer – whereas there are many shades of grey in questions such as "Are you set up for success?" There is a level of comfort and simplicity when only binary answers are needed to progress to the next phase of product development. Many engineering managers have such a hard time managing the binary issues that they quite often don't even venture into the grey areas. In fact, most engineering managers are simply not trained to even think about these things.

Building good software is difficult. In fact, the very term 'soft'ware is a misnomer. It *sounds* as though it is unscientific and something that can be easily accomplished. We think it should more aptly be called 'Harderware'.

How People *Feel* makes a Difference

In part to raise this type of awareness, most companies have a set of corporate values that are to be used as guiding principles in value based decision making. However, they are often not fully practiced and woven into the very fabric of everyday habits. In the hurry of fast software iterations, we forget about how people feel and that engineers need nurturing in this hectic environment. So, there is this untapped force – the soul of the software team – that has the potential to transform your business.

The soul and spirit of the team is influenced by many factors: the leadership, the organizational setup, the physical environment, and whether the team believes that what they are doing is worthwhile, whether they have a voice in decision making and whether they feel they are set up for success. How people *feel* impacts how productive and committed they are to the organizational goals – and ultimately this has a significant impact on the products developed and released by the group.

The spirit of the team is very much like the roots of a tree. It is hidden. Yet, it is the source of the team's ongoing strength and energy. A deep set of roots can nurture a healthy, strong tree that can yield an abundance of fruits, and withstand many storms. Growing such a tree is really the art of inspiring the software soul. It takes time, patience and energy. The results can be a huge boost to creating good software more predictably and with higher, sustained profitability. Ultimately, you reap what you sow.

REAL ENGINEERS DON'T WORK IN SOFTWARE FACTORIES

The term "software factory" was coined in the late sixties to describe how software can be created predictably and reliably through an assembly line process – analogous to factories that manufacture tangible goods.

The notion that software could be assembled in this way has appeal: it simplifies the building of software to predictable smaller pieces that can then be integrated into a larger solution. Much of this concept has been put into use and has shaped the software development process as we know it today. However, as we saw in the previous chapter, a focus on only the software development process and traditional metrics are not sufficient to make the huge productivity leaps.

Real engineers simply cannot thrive in software factories. They need a nurturing and creative environment to foster their spirit and propel them to accomplish great things. This "magic energy" is missing in the software factory environment. Business owners that want to create innovative, high quality products reliably and profitably need to expand their vision of how to tap into the talents and spirits of this workforce.

Real software engineers – software *artists* – need to be *inspired* to do the right thing. This is only possible with a strong cultural foundation that nurtures the spirit of the software teams. And, what does that nurturing really entail?

The next section describes a story which illustrates the role of software culture in shaping business outcome. This story is a composite of many discussions and interviews.

It is an *extreme* case in that everything that can go wrong does go wrong. It describes the many pitfalls that an engineering team faces when trying to deliver a software product.

One of the interviewees who inspired this story said "A few years ago, I was a new manager. I was really excited to be promoted to management, but I regretted taking the role after a couple of months. I was unprepared to deal with the people drama. It took up more of my time than dealing with the technical challenges. I was really frustrated. As silly as it sounds, I felt I could have done a better job of shipping the product if it weren't for the people. Obviously, I needed to become a better people manager. I think if we paid more attention to the people issues – such as hiring the right leaders, and supporting them – that would go a long way in enabling success."

The point of this extreme story is to illustrate the many pitfalls in the software engineering environment. Following the story is a summary of the 'lessons learned' from which a framework is proposed for enabling software success.

DAVID AND HIS SOFTWARE ADVENTURE

Executive management has decided to invest in building a next-generation software product "Product Z". They decide to form the team under David. David is known as a very technical and energetic senior engineer and he is deemed to be ready for management. David is seen as a technical expert in his area: he handles the most complex areas of work; he is known to be highly productive and has the highest bug-fix rate in the team. He is also known as the "go to guy" for critical customer issues and as a point of contact for other engineering teams.

While the other engineers think David is a reasonable engineer, they don't necessarily share management's views that he is solid or that he is ready for management. David's peers view him as someone who hacks, and then goes into the mode of massive bug-fixing – someone who is known to have good "diving catch" abilities. To top it off, David typically agrees to everything asked of him, which leads people think he is mainly out to please management and not really strong on engineering the right solution. What is commonly known to the grass roots is not known to the management team that decides to appoint David.

Management sees David as someone reliable, technical and someone with a "can-do" attitude. Besides, David might leave the group if they don't give him a promotion to manager soon. He has asked them many times for this opportunity. So David is appointed as the manager.

Management decides to help David out by seeding the team. They had been outsourcing much of their "running the business" activities to India so that they could staff an innovative project such as this in North America. Management identifies a team of five engineers whose component had transferred to India several months ago, and moves these engineers under David. They were reasonable engineers, but they will need training in the new technology. In addition, David is also given three engineers who are expert in the new technology areas needed to build the product. These three engineers would be the team anchor. They were known to be highly technical, and sharp. But, they also had a reputation for over-engineering solutions, being difficult to get along with, and not really getting things done. The team in a nutshell had three experts and five regular engineers – with David as the new manager for the project.

David quickly realized the challenges of his new team. Although he had a team of eight, only the three experts were able to engage in any real design discussions. The other five engineers were "fillers": they had to be trained in the new technology first. Besides, they were constantly being pulled into nightly calls and emergency support requests from the India team that had taken over their component. So, most of the design discussions took place with the three experts.

Very quickly, David realized that the requested content and timelines were simply impossible. The product was complex: it would require several prototypes, and iteration with end users, before developing a final product. His team of eight was not yet functioning at full capacity. In addition, these five engineers were becoming demoralized at not being able to participate in the design discussions for the new project and resentful of the fact that the "expert Prima donnas" did not share their knowledge.

The tensions were mounting within the team. People spent more time complaining than they did learning the new technology. He knew that with the elitist attitudes of the three experts and the grueling schedules of the five core engineers, the team could split apart at any moment. Even though David was a brand new manager, he realized that team morale and capacity were going to be critical in shaping the product.

David spent a lot of time with the team to calm things down and appease frustrations. He had to step outside his own comfort zone and talk to each of the engineers about how they felt, what they wanted, and how they can work together. David was frustrated this "people-stuff" took up so much time. He really wanted to just get the product built.

In reality, the team was not happy. The five core engineers had joined this team hoping to get more exposure to the new technology. However, they spent the majority of their time "babysitting" the new team in India. The early morning and late night meetings were also taking a heavy toll on their personal lives. Their repeated efforts to flag the issues to upper management were ignored. Why is it that after 6 months of transferring the technology, the India team still required so much hand holding? The ramp up was really slow. The offshore team's productivity looked good on paper, but all the "behind the scenes work" that was done by the North American team was not accounted for. The extra effort of the five engineers made the offshore engineers productivity look great and at the same time was starting to seriously impact schedules for the next-gen product.

Managers above David only saw was that the "India strategy was working well and improved operational efficiencies". The engineers on the ground might as well have been reading the National Enquirer. David empathized with the engineers, but was unable to convince his upper management of the deep troubles so evident to the grass roots. The executives did not want to listen to feedback that contradicted their strategy. The layers of delusion were simply incredulous! This deepened the engineers' mistrust of management's ability to make sound decisions.

The three Prima donna experts had their own set of issues. They distrusted each other. There were frequent emotional outbursts at technical meetings, heated email exchanges, mysterious absences, and slammed doors. Things were explosive between the troublesome trio – and David had his hands full trying to get them to behave and work together. David was annoyed at how much time the team took from him to actually make them behave. David and his team struggled to work together, and muddled their way through all the unhappiness and friction. It was an ongoing struggle for David to keep his team under some level of control: after all, he did not sign up to be a psychologist. He just wanted to build something cool.

David worked hard. With the help of his experts, he pulled together the product roadmap. The management wanted ten key features, by March. David was projecting that he would be able to deliver a proof of concept in March with three core features; and, he projected a Production Release in the following year. This was the best he and his lead engineers could come up with – and it was quite aggressive at that.

The day of the big roadmap review arrives. David presents the projected product implementation timeline and feature content. This is where David had to communicate the reality of what is possible vs. PowerPoint dreams. The room explodes in discussion, with one pointed question after another coming from the executives. They cannot believe that the product could not be built as per their forecasts. They quiz David on each of his assumptions to see how much more content can be squeezed with the existing headcount. The bully management style works to some extent. David reluctantly agrees to add another feature and bring in the timeline by two months.

All in all, the review did not go well. The executives were not happy with David's proposal, and in their efforts to "help", they added more complexity to a plan that was already on shaky ground.

By the time the roadmap review ended, the executives had left David with a truly impossible task. He had come into the review hoping to get glory for his heroic efforts in *devising a very aggressive plan and get kudos for doing so despite the resource and technical challenges. Instead, the execs had bullied him into accepting a ridiculous timeline with an impossible set of roadmap items. The executives were not willing to listen to the challenges.*

David thought software managers were supposed to provide inputs on what is possible before decisions were made. He was not prepared to deal with the "just go do what I have decided" attitude. David's respect for the executives diminished. The executives were puzzled by David's sudden negative attitude. They expected better from David.

David and his team were emotionally drained even before starting the design phase of their product. None of them felt that they were set up for success. Their beliefs were further reinforced by the roadmap review and subsequent program reviews. Each review focused on how the team was executing to a plan that made no sense, with an organization that was not set up for success, with engineers that could not work with each other and a leader who was unprepared to lead. The team's morale suffered considerably and yet somehow they went through the motions of building the product.

The Adventure Concludes

So, how did this story end? The product shipped about a year late with about half the requested features. It made a big splash and contributed reasonably to the company's quarterly revenues. So, in some sense the product succeeded.

On the other hand, there were also a number of issues. There were a huge number of customer found defects in the product, and it was difficult to use. Although customers were open to buying the first incarnation of the product, they provided feedback that subsequent sales would depend on a more comprehensive feature-set and superior quality and usability. The company had to triple its investment to enhance and support the product. There was a high attrition rate in the original team of engineers – with many of them noting morale, lack of trust, inability to make a difference, and chaotic work environment as key factors for their departures. The engineers also noted that the product had some fundamental quality issues that were deep-rooted in short-cuts that were taken to meet dates. The engineers were not proud of the product they had delivered. The engineers that were left behind were deeply unhappy and were continuously looking for a way out. So, there was an even higher cost to the company in bringing in a constant stream of new engineers to continue with the product development.

The actual profit gain was questionable, and the customer satisfaction suffered. And, because they had to invest heavily in the maintenance and support of the new product, the company had to cut back on innovation in other areas.

At the end of the year, product Z looked very similar to the legacy product David had been working on when he was promoted. Management put a quality program in place in get things in shape. They knew David had experience with getting things in shape quickly – perhaps they had the right leader in place after all. David did a great job once more in the diving catches and trained his entire team to follow suit. However, they still continued on a downward spiral. The company started to look at other alternatives to compete in the market.

LESSONS FROM DAVID'S ADVENTURE

This story is a composite of many such stories we heard. The software world is full of projects like Project Z: many of these projects also shared the same fate. Setting up the right leadership, supporting them, and addressing the concerns of the engineering teams are all critical factors in enabling success. Another of our interviewees said "Hiring the right leader is absolutely critical. I have worked for many engineering managers who were not interested in managing people, and the entire project suffers".

Software projects are hit and miss because we often forget to pay attention to the people dimension. First, the right leader needs to be hired. Obviously, David was not qualified for this role. In addition, the engineering manager and team need to *believe* they are set up for success: listening to their inputs, having open discussions and working together to remove roadblocks makes a huge difference to team spirit. We often miss opportunities to take the team inputs into account when making decisions – because of the "software rush".

The pace of software iterations is fast; we pay attention to milestones and metrics and sometimes forget to take into account the real sentiments of the software team. We especially dismiss the team inputs when what they have to say contradicts the plans initially set forth. When we forget this dimension, we lose the spirit of the software team – and lose the opportunity to achieve greater business impact. We also miss the real benefits of iterative development – which is continuous learning, and the ability to refine plans as we move along. This iterative learning includes learning about the project via traditional checkpoints and metrics, as well as continuously monitoring and getting qualitative and emotional feedback from the software team.

If the spirit is not there, if the team does not believe in what they are doing, then that needs to be addressed. Listening to the concerns of the team and making adjustments takes time, but it pays off. Having the right leader in place is critical to make this transition.

Listening to the grassroots team may seem to be counter-productive as it can slow down decision-making. One engineering manager made the point "If you listen to the engineers, every project will be cancelled before it takes off". This view has some validity; an organization can get into a mode of "paralysis by analysis".

However, it is essential to strive for a middle ground and hear out all points of view. Having the hearts and minds of the grassroots engineering team behind the project is a key factor in propelling project success.

The Socio-Organizational Fabric

Catching "socio-organizational issues" early and monitoring them on an ongoing basis is critical to staving off negativity and *inspiring* software teams to greater success and maximum business impact. Strong teams, with strong spirit are more likely to be able to withstand the many challenges of software development and drive the creation of stronger, more resilient and profitable products.

Sustainable profitability means building strong teams, with strong cultures – deep roots that fuel the team to create amazing products each and every time. This is the magic of a strong cultural foundation.

Setting the overall tone for execution and enabling a strong engineering culture is absolutely critical. There are some key ingredients required to enable software success:

strong leadership, organizational setup, physical proximity, healthy working relationships, trust, and values that are practiced in everyday decisions. This is the cultural fabric of the organization. The culture is shaped by its leaders: CEO's, VP's, Directors and engineering managers. It is tempting to ignore this "fluffy cultural stuff" and just maintain a singular focus on the more traditional software success metrics: release content, schedules, test results, and bug-fix metrics. A singular focus on the visible, without enough attention on the more intangible measures, almost always results in deep fissures that impact the long term viability of the product and the software team.

For example, if there were regular checkpoints on team dynamics, organizational effectiveness, and openness of communication, Product Z would have ended up with a more stable infrastructure and a proud engineering team; the company may have made more money in doing things right from the start and retained its top talent for the next round of innovations. We have heard many such "turn-around", inspiring stories and will share these with you throughout the book. These are the ingredients of the "secret sauce" that can either propel your teams to software success or shackle them in endless quality and productivity issues resulting in poor profits.

The next section will establish a framework for enabling these core ideas and weaving them into the cultural fabric of your software teams.

FRAMEWORK FOR SOFTWARE SUCCESS

As we saw from the case study, the traditional focus on time to market, product content and revenues will not necessarily lead to sustained software success. In fact, a sharp focus on just these outwardly-visible success factors can lead to fissures in the spirit of the software team, and deeper systemic issues, resulting in poor quality, innovation breakdown, and talent loss. That in turn has a direct impact on your competitive advantage and profits. It is clear that another set of core elements are at work: the elements that shape the cultural dynamics of the team.

We have ridden the software revolution by its sheer newness – there was so much ground to cover. So, simply looking at the basic metrics was deemed sufficient. These are metrics we are all familiar with by now: time to market, product content, quality metrics and revenues. As we enter into the third decade of software commercialization, it has become important to also optimize and fully leverage our software teams. To do that requires expanding our views and including other measures of success that directly impact the happiness and productivity of software teams – that is, the very soul of our teams. This category of things includes deeper ideas such as: organizational culture, leadership, values, and emotional health. Happier software teams are more productive and have a large positive impact on your business.

The following table depicts the characteristics we typically use to measure a successful software product and the deeper characteristics of the organizational culture that energize the software soul.

Product Success Factors

Enablers for great products

- Revenues
- Customer Satisfaction
- Time to market
- Feature Rich Products

Organizational Success Factors

Enablers for a great software culture

- Nurturing Leadership
- Close knit community
- Software soul
  - Atmosphere, values, energy
- People-Focused Operations
  - Putting values into action

A strong foundation of these deeper values is essential to keep your organization happy and productive and fully leverage the strength in your software teams. You may think that this framework applies to any industry – so, what is so special about software? The challenge with software is that good software skills are rare. Highly technical people are hard to find – let alone highly technical people that can get products out the door.

Organizational skills are seldom overtly valued in the software culture. There is "bully management", flame mails, hacks, and organizational warfare – and it is tolerated, because the people involved are deemed too critical and too difficult to discipline. Software leaders and engineers *are* a difficult lot. When they eventually get promoted to the higher ranks in companies, their influence extends far and wide and what could have been a fairly contained problem becomes more widespread – and before you know it the software culture as we know it today is created.

The story of David's Adventure is an example of how serious the problem is. Companies and organizations can still get by. But it is like running a marathon with 10 pound weights attached to your ankles. You may be able to pull through, but, most likely, you will fail. If you do win, there will be tremendous pain. Is it high time to start thinking about removing the shackles?

SOFTWARE BUSINESS DIAGNOSTICS

This would be a good point for you to baseline how your software business is faring across key measures of product and organizational success factors.

Before beginning this diagnosis, ask yourself "how much do you really care about the welfare of your software team"? This may seem to be an odd question. If you have read the book this far, chances are you probably care. A software engineering manager plays a pivotal role in the success of their teams. Being tuned into the overall team pulse, their needs and what it takes to motivate them requires continuous attention and your presence. That is, you really need to be engaged and involved in managing your teams. It can't be done in your spare time, after taking care of your projects. It comes from a realization that the success of your software engineering team is tied to your personal success as an engineering manager and to the overall business success. Once you have internalized this, then you are ready to open your mind and read the rest of the book.

Now let's discuss how to start diagnosing the state of your business, taking into account the organizational success factors – which are critical to the energy of the software soul.

David's organization created Product Z and several of the traditional software-success measures were good. The team was able to build a product, with a reasonable set of features, and reap reasonable revenues. The company proved that they could deliver Product Z on time and capture a critical part of a new market. However, there were fissures in the organization: lack of teamwork, lack of open communications, poor leadership, no pride of ownership, and attrition. As a result, the quality, profitability and innovation for the product and the organization were jeopardized. The net results simply do not add up and even more investment would be required to shore up the product.

Pick a software team and a product they own, and rate it across these categories. Then, think about what can be done to strengthen the net result and long term profitability.

Here is a table that lists these attributes for David's Product Z and his overall organization. The scale is from 1-5, with 1 being low and 5 being high.

How does your organization fare in the framework?

Product: success factors	David's Product Z	Your Product
Revenue	3	
Customer Satisfaction	3	
Time to Market	5	
Features	3	
Organizational Success factors	**David's organization**	**Your organization**
Nurturing Leadership	2	
Close-knit community	2	
Software Soul: Atmosphere, values, energy	2	
People-focused operations	2	
Costs	**Sustained results: product Z**	**Sustained results: your product**
Support, & Maintainability	5	
Innovation starvation	5	
Talent Attrition	5	
Organizational Flux	5	

It is obvious that the costs are significant for Product Z and that the main reasons are failures in the organizational culture.

Simply put, productivity is maximized by focusing on not just product success – but, also organizational success. And organizational success, with a strong culture fosters great products, innovation and retains top talent. The productivity equation translates to:

Productivity = Benefit / Cost

Benefit = Product Success + Organizational Success

Increased organizational success leads to reduced costs

The effect of organizational success is compounded:

- reduced costs
- increased benefits

Following these principles leads to greater productivity and ultimately to greater profitability for the company.

The rest of the book delves into the four major factors that shape software culture that enable organizational success and light the software soul.

These factors are:

- **Leadership Ecosystem**
  - o Setting up a strong leadership framework
- **The Community**
  - o Building Strong, Fun teams
- **The Software Soul**
  - o Energizing, Inspiring atmosphere
- **People-Focused Operations**
  - o Infusing people focus into team operations

These factors can be depicted as follows:

We will explore these four major factors, and how you can create an organizational culture that unleashes the maximum potential of your software engineering team. Harnessing the power will result in transforming your product lifecycle, increased productivity, innovative solutions, and energized teams.

Your bottom line will benefit by tapping into the soul of your software teams.

Section 2

Leaders

Seeds of Inspiration and Values

"A leader takes people where they want to go. A great leader takes people where they don't necessarily want to go, but ought to be" ... Rosalynn Carter

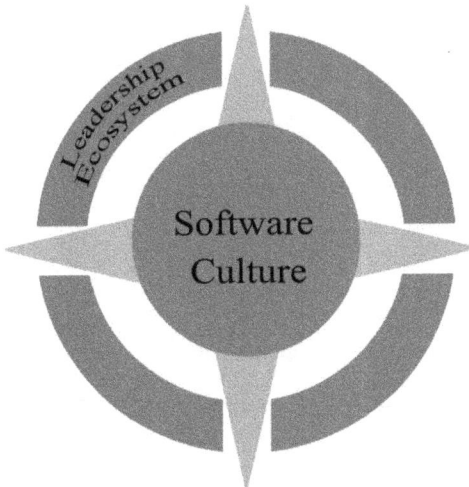

THE CULTURAL ATOM

Great software culture is critical for sustained success and productivity. An organization where there is a high level of trust, teamwork and enthusiasm will naturally produce greater results than one where there is constant friction. However, such an organization seems difficult to find in the engineering world. Most of the people we interviewed told horror stories about their teams and their managers and felt that their full potential was not leveraged.

You may wonder why such dysfunction is so commonplace in engineering. Engineers work well with machines and logic. They have a very deep sense of what is fair, and how they should be rewarded and recognized for their work. For the most part, engineers are competitive and have ranked consistently at the top of their class in order to gain entry into engineering or computer science. After that, they go through rigorous interviews to get into a company. So, they naturally expect to be "above average" most of the time.

Just because a team comprises several above average, logical people does not mean they will produce above average results. This is because the engineers need to work within an organizational culture and framework. How they are enabled and set up within that framework makes all the difference in whether the team succeeds or fails and whether a software project succeeds or fails. To create sustained productivity and success in a software team, you need to tap into everyone's full potential and enable them to work together in a cohesive team. And, to do that, you need to foster a strong culture, and tap into everyone's emotional energy.

How do you create a great software culture? Great cultures are created by great leaders. They in turn are enabled by the right organizational framework, hire other great leaders, create cohesive teams and inspire them to greatness. In an engineering organization, engineering managers play a pivotal role: they hold the atomic unit of execution and delivery – the engineering team. In effect, they are the cultural atom. Having an organization of strong engineering managers is critical to the success of the overall organization.

Wanted: More than Technical Virility!

Good engineering managers need to possess a fine balance of technical skills, operational skills and people skills. More than anything, they need to be motivated to make a difference in shaping engineering culture. There are many engineers who are motivated to become managers because they see that as the only path to move ahead in their careers. I have personally counseled many to only enter the field if they have a *real* interest and desire to work on people problems in addition to technical problems. It can't be just about a "race for titles" – but a genuine interest in building great teams and unleashing the full potential of engineers.

Selecting an engineering manager is a very critical decision. The engineering manager is the only manager in the organization that has direct access to tangible results produced by engineers. Everyone above that level is managing expectations and integrating pieces of various products.

The following story illustrates the criticality of the engineering manager and different skills needed to create a strong engineering team. It also illustrates the role of executives in hiring and supporting the engineering manager and their team through times of transition.

The interviewee who inspired this story was asked to talk about how an engineering manager can impact team success. She said "Let me tell you about a team I worked in a few years ago. My manager was running us ragged. Our team was always struggling, and we did not have a good reputation. I think the fact that our manager did not have the support of the executives had a role to play in this. It had a negative impact on the entire team. I felt like we were running on a treadmill without getting anywhere. I didn't think I could make a difference and wanted to leave. In fact, everyone was always on the lookout for another job. Then, they brought in a new manager and things changed for the better. She set the right expectations, brought in staffing changes and really engaged with the team. She also had support from the executives. That made it a lot easier for her to get her job done and things started to improve. I wish these changes had happened a lot sooner".

Bill and Mary - cultural atoms in action

Bill was the manager of Team, XYZ, comprised of eight engineers. The output of the team was mediocre: the feature velocity was low, the quality was poor and there were many customer escalations. Bill's team of eight engineers had three high flying gurus, two low performers and three junior engineers. Bill was known to be technical, aggressive and able to get things done. In other words, he was the classic, technically virile engineering manager.

However, the team was barely meeting their targets, and in fact their throughput was declining over time. Bill worked the gurus to the max but did very little to manage the others. Bill thought they were weak and did not try to challenge or grow them. Neither did he let them go. They lingered in the team. They did as they were told, but nothing more. Also, from Bill's perspective, even the most mediocre engineers would be hard to replace. After all, they each knew some part of the code base, and having them in the team enabled some level of progress. As a result, the top engineers ended up doing all the heavy lifting, and burned out. They did not feel inspired to do their best. They became frustrated, and left the team. The engineers that were left behind were not trained to think independently. Whenever they had tried to engage in design discussions, Bill had quickly shut them down in favor of having them "just implement". They were just programmer-bots, not engineers. The quality declined rapidly due to Bill's mismanagement.

The executives had been monitoring throughput of the team in various program meetings, and became alarmed when the targets declined rapidly. They replaced Bill with Mary.

Mary took over team XYZ. It was in shambles. There were no expert engineers in the team. There were a multitude of feature requests and quality goals to meet – but no one to do the job! Mary was brought into the organization by the Vice-President, who had worked with her on an earlier assignment and had been impressed with her ability to build great teams. She was also highly regarded technically and had a knack for just getting things done. Although the team was short three engineers, she knew that the remaining five were not fully leveraged. She was able to hire two strong engineers based on her personal reputation for being a good manager. She also fired the two weakest performers. She knew that they had been in cruise control for some time and the effort involved to turn them around would likely not result in success quickly.

The team was much smaller than before – five instead of eight. Mary discussed the situation with her upper management, and informed them that she needed some "air cover": that is, she needed at least six months to get things in shape, and solicited her management to reset client expectations. The executives were somewhat reluctant, but in the end they agreed to shave off all but the most critical deliverables from the team. Mary's personal reputation with the Vice-President made it easier to get this sponsorship. This gave Mary some breathing space and she focused on rebuilding the team. Mary held several team-building sessions and modified the team operations. She asked everyone to come prepared for design and code reviews, expected everyone to participate and expected good quality work on time. She also encouraged open debate and discussion and helped the team explore alternate solutions to problems – and thereby increase their general excitement. She provided regular feedback and asked senior engineers in other teams to mentor her engineers. In effect, she cajoled, and motivated her team by actively engaging in their daily operations, paying attention to detail and demanding excellence. There was no tolerance for "can't do attitudes", "missed deliveries" and sloppy work.

With this much higher standard in place, Mary was able to inspire her team to a higher level of achievement. The team of five was able to do a lot more than Bill's team of eight. The momentum she built also attracted other top engineers. With a strong team in place, Mary was able to bring things under control in 6 months. After a year, Mary's team had gained the confidence of the client and partner teams and was executing on both features and quality goals. In addition, employee morale had significantly improved, and some of the engineers had even started thinking about applying for a patent.

Lessons from Bill & Mary - Atomic Power

The impact of engineering managers is clearly seen in the above example. They can make or break a software team and a software project. They can set a high standard for project execution, the behaviors that are valued, and the general energy of execution. A good engineering manager can maximize the power of a team, create a happy and cohesive team, and bring about greater productivity. Hence, it is imperative to select engineering managers with care. They are the cultural atoms from which the much larger organizational cultural fabric is built.

It is absolutely critical to get the right leaders in place in a software organization. The software engineers are highly paid, scarce resources. Each member of a software team is hard to replace. The more complex projects require more training time and it can take an average of about 6 months for a software engineer to become productive in their domain. It can also take a significant amount of a senior engineer's time to train a new hire. So, hiring and replacing engineers is an expensive undertaking.

Bill's mismanagement had significant negative impact on the business:

- Attrition and talent loss
- Productivity loss
- Delayed roadmap and delivery timelines
- Delayed product release and lost customer confidence

This is perhaps the single distinguishing factor between managing software engineers and managing factory workers. They are scarce, expensive resources, take time to train, are hard to replace and they are not fungible. Engineering is a specialized skill and managing engineers is an even more specialized skill.

Why did Mary's management style work when Bill's did not? Mary and Bill essentially had the same group of engineers. In fact, Mary had only a subset – both in terms of numbers and skill set. One key difference is that Mary actively managed the performance and expectations of the engineers in her team. Her personal energy and active participation enabled Mary to build the right culture in the team and turn things around. Mary was present and engaged with her team. Another point to note is Mary actively solicited upper management support and won their sponsorship – without which it would have been impossible to affect the turnaround. As much as the engineering manager has a role to play, executives have an even more important role in the selection of the engineering manager and their ongoing sponsorship of that person.

TRAITS OF SUCCESSFUL ENGINEERING MANAGERS

Let's have a closer look at the traits of a successful engineering manager. How do you go about selecting a good engineering manager? What qualities should you look for? Here is a list that we compiled based on our many interviews:

1. **Technical Aptitude, focus and drive**
   - Strong analytical and problem solving skills
   - Strong technical judgment
   - Reputation for delivering high quality products on time
   - Accountability and reliability
   - Customer focus: A good understanding of how their technology can be leveraged in the customer environment
   - Strong work ethic, passion and drive

2. **Operational Excellence**

   - Manage project scheduling, tracking and execution
   - Create balanced product portfolio
   - Optimize resources: use the least number of resources to address maximum number of business needs
   - Customer focus: A good understanding of how their technology can be leveraged in the customer environment

3. **People and communications skills**

   - Connecting with their team and inspiring them to greatness

- Creating a strong sense of community and purpose
- Being fair in project assignments and rewards
- Performance management: attracting top employees and letting go of weaker ones
- Fostering pride of ownership, creativity and innovation
- Soliciting concerns and feedback & taking actions
- Establishing a career path for their team members

4. Fit into the leadership ecosystem & Sponsorship

- Gaining the sponsorship of their management
- Connecting with their peers
- Collaborating with other teams
- Gaining customer trust
- Assessing and Navigating office politics

We found that there were differences in the traits seen in engineering managers. The more successful managers had strong technical skills and operational skills, but also excellent people skills and sponsorship from the management.

The traits most typically sought out by executives in an engineering manager are:

- Strong technical aptitude, focus and Drive
- Operational excellence

The traits most valued by engineers in their manager are:

- Strong technical aptitude, focus and Drive
- Operational excellence
- People and communications skills

The traits of the most successful engineering managers are:

- Strong technical aptitude, focus and Drive
- Operational excellence
- People and communications skills
- Fit into the leadership ecosystem

Managers are most often hired based on their technical aptitude and operational excellence. They most often fail if they cannot master "People and communication skills" and they certainly will not be promoted without "Sponsorship or fit into the leadership ecosystem". If the leaders fail, the teams fail, the projects fail and the organization fails. So, it is critical to choose the leader that has the best chance to succeed in *all three* areas. This is illustrated in the diagram below:

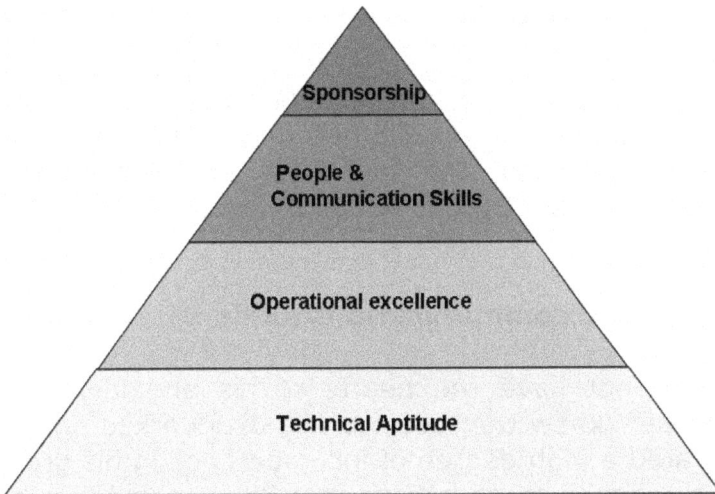

Traits of Successful Engineering Managers

Bill and Mary – Success Factors

Let's look at the example of Mary and Bill discussed earlier:

What leadership traits did Mary have that helped her succeed? Let's do a comparison based on our success hierarchy:

Strong technical aptitude, focus and Drive

Both Bill and Mary were strong in this area. They were both respected by their teams for their technical knowledge, and being results focused.

Operational Excellence

Bill was weak in this area. He was unable to balance his product portfolio between sustaining and feature delivery. This started exhibiting itself in the team's inability to deliver. Also, the team was not optimized. Many of the engineers in the team were not working at full potential. Hence, Bill's team of eight was really functioning at the level of a team of maybe four or five.

Mary on the other hand was able to successfully and optimize the resources. She leveraged only five engineers to do the same job as Bill had done with eight. She also further balanced the portfolio by eliminating some deliverables so that she could focus on rebuilding the team.

People and communications skills

Bill did not have the hearts of his engineers. His lead engineers knew they were being overworked and that Bill tolerated a high degree of incompetence in his group. This led the engineers to believe that Bill was unfair in his work distribution and rewards. Eventually, the lead engineers left the group. His senior staff did not feel trusted or inspired to do their best. His junior staff was scared to question his authority – even though they often had valid technical concerns. Obviously Bill was not able to foster a culture of trust, and community within his team. Instead he used his technical superiority to bully his team into action. As a result, the team got things done – but only whatever they were told to do. Each of them was also busy looking for their next job and doing the absolute minimum to keep the project moving along. Bill had lost the hearts of the engineers, and therefore he was only able to leverage a small percentage of their minds. Bill was never able to reap the full potential of his team.

Mary was able to build confidence and loyalty in her team. She actively performance managed her group and let go of the two weakest engineers. This sent a signal that she was aware of which engineers were good and which ones were coasting. In addition, she put in place process changes and actively participated in working through the changes with her team. For example, she sat in on design and code reviews and gave constructive input. This demonstrated in a tangible way what her expectations were and that she was "on their side". Her decisive actions to improve the overall health of the team garnered her respect and backing from her engineers.

Fit into the leadership ecosystem & Sponsorship

Bill was not connected with the larger leadership ecosystem. He was focused intensely on the technical execution and delivery and missed some basic people management issues. The only venue for executives to connect with Bill was through the program reviews. As such, they were not clued into the dysfunctional nature of Bill's team until the results from Bill's team were starting to deteriorate. Clearly, the delayed realization that Bill's team was ineffective could have been mitigated if there was a stronger "people connection" and awareness between upper management, Bill and Bill's staff. That is, there needed to be ongoing communications about how Bill was leading the team, and how the team was doing – in addition to how the results looked at program reviews. This awareness is the first step in making changes. It could have resulted in coaching for Bill, or replacing Bill with a more effective manager earlier. Bottom line is that the leadership ecosystem could have had a net positive impact on business results: prevent the departure of key engineers, replace Bill earlier and essentially nip issues in the bud before they crop up as issues in the program review and start impacting business commitments.

Mary sought out a connection with her management. She knew that in order for her to turn around the team, she would need their help. She asked for air cover from her management to reset customer expectations. This single but important act of sponsorship gave her some time to bring in new talent, reset expectations within the team, and build the necessary momentum. The fact that her management team sponsored her plan made all the difference. It is rare that sponsorship is as easily gained as in Mary's case. Mary's case was actually helped by the fact that she had a solid reputation with one of the executives in her chain of command – and her recommendations were seriously considered. However, without this, the team would have languished even more and spiraled into a state of complete disrepair. Instead, Mary was able to affect the turnaround within six months, regain customer confidence and start having a positive business impact.

Cultural Atom Fuels Success

The example of Bill and Mary illustrates the importance of choosing an engineering manager wisely and the role of executives in setting them up for success. It has an impact on your bottom line and business profitability. The right leader, with the right people skills and sponsorship, can make the difference between an unsuccessful, struggling team and one that sizzles. In this example, fostering a people-oriented culture, putting in place effective people-managers, and monitoring "leadership effectiveness" would have gone a long way to mitigate the issues. There is typically a lag between when "people issues" emerge and when they begin to impact projects. There is an intervening period of time where things can be turned around without too much impact. Once troubling signs start showing up in program metrics, it is already too late to react without having an impact on the project and the long term viability of the functional area. The best way to manage engineering leaders and their teams is by *ongoing* monitoring of results, business metrics *as well as* their emotional well-being and connection to the overall organizational culture and goals.

Many of these traits may seem somewhat basic and not necessarily unique to engineering managers. However, it is important to note that many engineering managers are promoted into management based on technical skills and project management skills. People management and soft skills generally do not come naturally to this group of individuals. Soft skills in an engineering manager are seldom valued or rewarded. Hence, they often lack the sponsorship to rise and have a broader impact. The net effect is that the majority of engineering managers lack good people skills and upper management support to have optimal impact.

The next chapter will examine the role of the leadership ecosystem in more depth, and how it influences team potential and business success.

THE LEADERSHIP ECOSYSTEM

An ecosystem is a closed-loop system of living things that interact with each other and their environment continuously. It provides the support and balance to nurture the growth of everything in its sphere.

The leadership ecosystem is the framework through which the entire leadership organization – executives down to engineering managers – connects with the hearts and emotions of their staff, and optimizes their interactions for success. The key elements of this framework are:

- Hiring the right engineering manager
- Building a strong Leadership Web
    - Sponsoring its leaders
    - Fostering peer networks
    - Minimizing bureaucracy

In the last chapter, we discussed the qualities of good engineering managers. This chapter will discuss how engineering managers also need a supporting ecosystem to thrive and make a strong business impact.

We will look at each of these aspects in the following sections.

SPONSORSHIP

Setting up the right organizational framework and putting the right leaders in place is most critical in a software engineering organization. The organization's leaders weave the cultural fabric and build a strong, vibrant culture where innovation thrives and engineers strive to do their best each day.

However, in order for these leaders to be effective, they need to feel *sponsored* in their roles. That is, they need to believe that upper management will help them succeed. The engineering manager, as the cultural atom of the organization, has an enormous influence on the engineering team. They can make a team of engineers feel proud and excited, and energize them to higher levels of productivity and innovation. If they feel they are not sponsored, the resulting problems stemming from lack of senior management support will almost always lead to discontent, unproductive teams and ultImately impact product development, delivery and profitability.

So what exactly do we mean by sponsorship? Sponsorship is when your upper management works *with* you, supports you and ultimately advocates your cause: for example, by providing guidance, acting as a trusted sounding board, and removing roadblocks. Each leader needs sponsorship from their management chain in order to succeed. Sponsorship is essential in building a strong partnership and trust between an engineering manager and their immediate management chain. This strong partnership allows for the team to "battle together" – rather than spend their time battling each other. A sponsored engineering manager is more likely to succeed. Hence, his team is also more likely to succeed and as a result, the entire company benefits from having loyal, dedicated and happy employees.

Happy leaders, with the right level of support and sponsorship can have much greater influence, sway and ability to get things done. They and their teams are also more likely to be recognized and rewarded for their accomplishments. This in turn fuels more good behavior. So, the key is to set in place the framework – the leadership web – that will enable the engineering managers to work cooperatively with their management, their peers and with the organization to maximize the throughput of their teams.

We will now look at a couple of examples that illustrate the importance of sponsorship in shaping business outcome. The first example is about Linda, a smart talented manager, who lacked sponsorship; the second example is about Harry, who was not just smart and talented, but also sponsored.

Linda inspired this story, with the following insight shared during the interview. The topic being discussed was how to succeed as an engineering manager. She said "I thought that as long as I did a good job and was able to deliver, that's all that mattered. I completely missed the need to connect with my own management. Getting sponsorship is extremely important. Of course, in my case, that was really hard to do – my manager seemed a bit intimidated by me. I think he really did not like having a strong manager work for him. You know, type B managers are only comfortable with type B employees. Without sponsorship, you cannot succeed – no matter how smart you think you are or how hard you work. So, I had no choice, but to move on."

Example: Linda's Lack of Sponsorship

Linda is the engineering manager of team ABC. She is known as a smart, capable manager who can get things done and is highly regarded across the company. Linda, however, feels that she is not sponsored by her management. On several occasions, Linda was not given credit for her work; there was no helping hand provided to remove roadblocks; and occasions when Linda was not listened to. In fact, her immediate manager Roy felt threatened by Linda. On more than one occasion, she challenged him publicly and he did not like to be challenged. Here is an example of how that fragile relationship between Linda and Roy played out in a particularly critical program.

Linda's project was coming up for an executive review and she held a dry run with Roy and some of his peers. Linda had pulled together a detailed proposal of the concept and execution plan. There were definitely some problem areas, and Linda wanted to use the dry run to discuss these points and figure out how some of the risks could be addressed. Linda really needed Roy's support to buy in to the plan and provide help in unblocking the key issues. Instead, Roy took the opportunity to challenge Linda on fundamental issues – such as the concept, the execution plans and timelines. In fact, Roy questioned her technical approach, challenged her assumptions and stated that the risks had not been fully thought out. Furthermore, he also did not believe that the problems Linda presented were real, and that the complexity of the work was not commensurate with the effort. Linda did not understand why Roy had not brought this up to her in private, and instead chose a critical public review to air his concerns for the first time.

The whole tone of the interaction was wrong: why would her immediate manager choose a public forum to bring up such concerns? Linda did not think any of Roy's arguments made much sense and was able to successfully defend her proposal. Linda was an expert in her area. Her success only fueled Roy's anger and displeasure. After all, Roy was her boss, and he was supposed to know better – it really did not look good for Linda to win the debate. Linda thought that Roy felt threatened by her confidence and knowledge of technical areas that he did not possess.

This meeting was yet another example of how Roy was clearly uncomfortable with Linda. The project itself passed the review. However, everyone (especially Linda) knew that there would be an ongoing uphill battle to get things done: there was complete lack of synergy between Roy and Linda and it was clear that Roy would continue to push back on Linda's ideas throughout the course of the project. The main battle of completing the project successfully would be eclipsed by Roy and Linda's battles. More time would be spent fighting with each other – rather than getting the job done.

Linda chose to simply ignore him as much as possible and start execution. However, it was very difficult for her to be effective without strong management support: there was no advocate for her project, no one to provide air cover and no one to recognize the results when they finally achieved their goals. It ended up as a hollow victory. As a result, Linda left the group shortly thereafter – as did some of her loyal engineers. The business suffered setbacks and losses as a result of this fractured relationship between Roy and Linda.

Here is an example of how sponsorship of Harry, the engineering manager, played a vital role in enabling success of a project. This story was conveyed through an interview with Stan, who was Harry's manager. Stan said the following about his management style. "I think a big factor in my team's success is that I only hire the best managers and then I trust them to do their jobs. You have to be secure enough to hire strong leaders – otherwise, you will simply have followers, not leaders. This has its drawbacks too. You will have lots of debates, and not everyone is going to agree with you just because you are the boss. So you need to be able to deal with that. Valuing feedback makes everyone feel like they are part of the decision. Mind you, I am not running a democracy – so, I make the final call. When I do, my rule is that everyone aligns. This has really helped me make better business decisions and build a loyal, spirited team over the years".

HARRY'S SPONSORSHIP PAVES THE WAY

Harry was responsible for project WXY. He knew this was a tough area that no had embarked on before and there would be many technical challenges. Harry worked with his team to identify the options and drafted a proposal. A project review was coming up – but, he wanted to get his manager Stan's view on the proposal. Stan had many engineering teams under him and he did not have time to delve into each area in great detail. He counted on his management team to do the detailed analysis and come up with proposals. He was always amazed at Harry's technical skills and wished he could be as much "on the ball". However, he knew the best he could do was to listen carefully and understand the proposal.

When Harry and Stan met, he was able to ask the probing questions in the private meeting and coached Harry to provide additional data or reword his ideas as appropriate. Harry could see that Stan was concerned, but he also made it clear that he was there to help. In fact, Stan had asked what he could do to help move this project forward. They brainstormed different alternatives, and as a result were able to come up with a joint plan that was far superior to Harry's initial proposal.

At the public project review meeting, Stan and Harry had to face the scrutiny of other management teams, but were able to present a unified front. Not only did the project pass the executive review, but Stan and Harry were also able to inspire confidence with the management staff that they will work through project issues together. Stan and Harry were able to work through problems together because they had a trusting relationship. The battle energy was saved for the inevitable technical problems that would arise and not for plotting against one another.

The trust and openness of the relationship between Harry and Stan made Harry feel like he was sponsored. He knew he could approach Stan with bad news, make proposals and ask for help. This ability to discuss problems openly and fight common battles strengthened their relationship and set a positive tone of operations within the team. All of Harry's team knew that Stan was a "good guy" and trying his best to help them succeed.

As a result, Harry was loyal to Stan. Because Harry was happy and confident, this spirit rubbed off on his team. The project had troubles, but they were able to work through the problems together. The strength of their relationships enabled them to work together without any hidden agendas. There was no finger pointing and one-upmanship. Everyone was heard, and the focus was problem solving.

The end result was a successful project and a successful team. The success in the team spirit and overall culture had lasting impact beyond just the single project.

Lessons in Sponsorship

What can we learn from the examples of Linda and Harry?

- Active sponsorship is critical

  Engineering managers need the active sponsorship of their management chain. This means establishing a joint vision, listening to concerns, removing roadblocks, and providing air cover.

- Debate privately, unite publicly

  Good engineering managers tend to be analytical, and have a pre-disposition to discuss, debate and question. Open, constructive debates between leaders can refine ideas and result in stronger business strategies, architectures and roadmaps.

  This should not be viewed as a threat – but a sign of a strong leadership team.

However, such debate should come to convergence and the leadership team needs to be unified in its communications.

Effective partnering between engineering managers and executives will boost the morale and productivity of the entire engineering team. Clients and partners have more confidence in a team that can stick together and support each other in public forums.

- Collaborate, don't compete

    The bench strength of your leadership team propels your own success. Managers should feel comfortable having staff that are stronger than them in select areas and be able to complement skills on the team. A collaborative framework between managers is critical to an organization's success. Managers that feel intimidated by their employees, like Roy, will surely drive away strong employees due to their own insecurities. In time, these organizations typically end up as hierarchies where there is fear, intimidation and lack of spirit – a sure fire way to scare of all your top notch engineers and leaders.

The key takeaway here is that a sponsored engineering manager is more effective and in turn can create a happy engineering team. And happy engineers build better products faster.

PEERS AND PARTNERS

It is difficult to be a "lone wolf" leader. Peer relationships at the leadership level are critical in fostering strong bonds and trust – which are a hallmark of a strong culture. These bonds are fundamental when working on any large projects – which almost always cross organizational boundaries. It is common knowledge that peer relationships are critical for managers to succeed. The point we want to make here is that executives also have a role to play in fostering peer relationships in their organization and beyond. The organizational structure, clarity of roles and responsibilities, and fair ownership are all key factors in shaping the peer network – and executives play an influential role in shaping these. Peer relationships need to be fostered so that everyone can play well together.

Consider an analogy to a symphony orchestra and the role of a conductor. Each musician specializes in their instrument and knows their role. But, the conductor needs to coordinate across the various teams and create the symphony. Played well, everyone succeeds. Played disparately, it just creates a lot of noise and everyone fails.

The following example illustrates how executives play a critical role in fostering strong peer relationships, and how it impacts the overall culture and influences business outcome.

This story was inspired by an interview with Don, who is Vice President at a mid size tech company. Don was especially proud of building a strong leadership team. His remarks were as follows. "I am really happy with my engineering organization. There is excellent cooperation and my leaders are energized. However, when I first came on board, things were in shambles. It took a while for me to figure out what was going on. It basically came down to the fact my management team did not feel empowered, and there was confusion over roles and responsibilities. Individually, the leaders were strong – but together, they were a disaster. Unfortunately, my predecessor had not fully engaged with his team. My sense is that he wanted the cachet of collaboration, but did not actively participate in making it successful. In fact, he left the team in a completely muddled state. So, I had my hands full in turning things around. As a senior leader, I think one of the values you bring is your ability to influence the behavior of other leaders and shape team dynamics. I think that has been a significant factor in my success and my team's success."

Example: Don Weaves the Web

Don was the Vice President of three engineering managers. He thought he had reasonable relationships with each of them and in turn he believed each of them worked well together. This was a big factor in how the entire team of engineers under Don felt like they were part of one large community. There were no silos; people were able to work in a give and take mode and help each other out. They were one big happy family. Other teams would often comment about how productive Don's team was. Don knew this was possible because each of his managers had built strong relationships with each other, and with their teams. There was an air of mutual respect, confidence and pride in the group that allowed them to overcome obstacles together.

It was not always like this. Don remembers the time when he first took over the group. None of the managers were communicating with each other. They were doing their own thing and the teams were muddling along. From the outside, they were viewed as a team that was slow to get things done, and where people seemed to do whatever they felt like. There were also severe attritions of top talent and an overwhelming number of under-performers that seemed to have crept into the team. All in all, the team was a mess. When Don took over the team, he held discussions with each of his direct managers. It was clear that there was a lot of duplicate and unnecessary work. Moreover, where it was important for the teams to work together toward a common goal, they struggled and could not come to agreement on a common vision, priorities or execution. Each manager mistrusted the other. In fact, they were in the midst this ongoing, simmering battle when Don took over. It was critical to turn things around.

Don started one-on-one discussions with his managers to understand what was going on. After a while, something emerged that seemed to be at the very root of the trouble. It seemed that Don's predecessor, Bill, had almost purposefully left things in a state of confusion. Bill did not want any one of his managers to fully own any project. Instead Bill held all managers jointly responsible for everything. This led to immense confusion of roles and responsibilities. The managers were each suspicious of the peers and instead of everyone helping out with everything – no one helped each other on any projects. Each manager took responsibility for whatever they thought was their responsibility and ran with it – with little regard for related areas. This had a direct impact on how the engineering teams functioned: there was inadvertent duplication of efforts, the engineers worked in silos, and they grew untrusting of engineers in their peer organizations. The team was living in an atmosphere of distrust and suspicion. It impacted morale, teamwork, and productivity. Most importantly, it impacted the bottom line of the business, which was spiraling downward under the cloud of pessimism. It took a while to bring all this out.

But, Don managed to get each manager to talk and put the pieces together.

To turn things around, Don called a one day offsite for his management team. The main purpose of the event was to build peer to peer relationships. He was sensitive to their highly tense relationships, and wanted to make sure he did not exacerbate things any further. Rather than start a discussion on feelings, he started with what he perceived to be the root of the problem: roles and responsibilities and lack of peer-to-peer communications. This framework allowed everyone to discuss the facts and in the course of the discussion, many more facts emerged about duplication, productivity loss and morale issues. This open dialogue allowed Don to reframe the roles and responsibilities within his management team and make it clear who was accountable for what. He also asked that the managers work on re-establishing their connections with each other and lead their teams by example. Once the managers realized that Don was on their side and wanted to help, they tried to make things work.

At subsequent one-on-one checkpoints, Don saw progressive improvements in communication between his managers. He also saw an increased level of trust between him and them. They seemed to know he cared and wanted to help. He continued to reinforce the importance of communications between the peer teams and actively worked to build trust between the managers. Certainly, having the clarity on roles and responsibilities helped tremendously. But, ongoing discussions on how each manager felt about their place in the organization, what role they wanted to play, and the level of trust and partnership between each other only helped to accelerate problem discovery and resolution. The pace at which the peer-to-peer fabric was repaired was accelerated, because everyone focused on it – and Don made it a priority.

This in turn helped the engineering managers to feel more confident about their roles and responsibilities. This new found confidence and positive outlook had enormous trickle-down impact on the overall engineering team. The engineers emulated their leaders and soon everyone was behaving as a cohesive team. The teamwork and morale improved considerably.

All this took about six months to achieve. But, Don made it a priority to repair the leadership web and focus on the peer to peer framework to unleash the power of the entire engineering team.

Leaders guide Collaboration

Don could have chosen to ignore the leadership web altogether. When coming into the team, what he saw was poor productivity and lack of accountability. He could have focused exclusively on the deliverables at hand, the bug count, and the other visible project metrics. By taking a bold step to look deeper into the problem, he discovered rips in the cultural fabric and was able to take measures to repair it. Don ended up with a team that could tackle any project – because they knew how to work together. He enabled a positive cultural change by engaging with his leadership team and fostering good relations. This made all the difference.

This story illustrates the importance to the business of strong peer networks. It also shows the critical role of the management leader, and how that person influences the collaborative spirit in the group. Any leader of managers should take an interest in setting up successful peer networks and fostering collaboration between their staff, partner teams and clients. When the peer network is strong, it fuels business success by boosting team morale and productivity – which ultimately results in a better product and a stronger team.

Beyond the Collaboration Cachet

In our many interviews, we found that there is a cachet attached to collaborative frameworks and decision making.

It is indeed a very critical ingredient in making software teams succeed. Yet, very few of these are effective. We heard time and again of failure patterns that lead to poor collaboration. Here are three common factors that contributed to poor collaboration and pitfalls to be aware of:

1. Lack of clear roles and responsibilities

Team members must have clear roles and responsibilities so that everyone understands what to expect from each other. When everyone has a defined role, insecurities are reduced, and it is easier to be part of the team. This results in more open communications, greater trust and collaboration. The example above illustrated the impact of having clear roles and responsibilities on the business results.

2. Significant variation in competence and accountability

Team members should have mutual respect for their competency in specific skills, and have a high degree of accountability to each other. Teams that comprise of individuals that cannot deliver or arc not compctent in the domains of interest will cause frustrations and slow everyone down.

The ideal situation is to have diverse, competent, accountable team members – where each person has respected strengths. Together the team can create something more than any one individual is capable of – that is the power of a strong collaborative team.

3. Lack of Executive Engagement

You can't simply throw a bunch of engineers and managers together and ask them to collaborate. When new programs, people and dynamics are brought together, things will inevitably take some time to sort out. Basics such as setting goals, roles, and deliverables take significant discussion. Executives have a critical role to play in setting up the team for success. They have to *participate* in the process. This is similar to Don's statement about how the previous VP "wanted the cachet of collaboration" but without the work. Most importantly, it takes patience and commitment to build a collaborative team.

BUREAUCRACY

As we discussed in previous sections, it is essential to choose the right engineering managers, provide sponsorship and build a leadership web across your organization. There is another key factor that impacts organizational effectiveness – bureaucracy. Bureaucracy can be a morale and productivity killer in engineering organizations. Knowing how much is sufficient to keep the organization humming versus having too much bureaucracy needs to be examined periodically.

Hierarchy & Leadership Density

Two factors that strongly influence bureaucracy are organizational hierarchy and leadership density.

Organizational hierarchy is the depth of a typical engineering reporting chain: does an engineer typically have three levels of management between himself and a VP or eight levels? The leadership density is the span of control per manager within this hierarchy. For example does each manager have at least seven direct reports and no more than fifteen?

Both of these factors (organizational depth and leadership density) have a direct impact on the organizational culture. The most notable aspect of their impact is on that quintessentially important area of interest to engineers ... bureaucracy. Simply put, bureaucracy needs to be lightweight in a software engineering organization. Software engineering relies on frequent iteration to build the product. Frequent short iterations enable a faster speed of engineering and increase productivity. Bureaucracy impedes frequent iteration. While it is important to have the right management within the leadership web, having too much management can really slow things down. So this is a critical area to consider in setting up your organization and projects for success.

We have all been in teams where the leadership density or hierarchy was off balance: the "too many cooks in the kitchen" problem. How did we feel? Typically, it was frustrating and slowed things down. The reason is simple. The greater the number of managers involved in a project, the longer it will take to arrive at a vision, make decisions, unblock issues and even get to the truth of what is really going on with a project. It is also easier to "pass the buck" when things go wrong, because no one is held fully accountable – and no one *feels* fully responsible.

Consider the following example where a VP expanded the scope of a project from one manager to four. Let's look at the impact on business outcome.

This story was inspired by an interview with Carla, an engineering manager, who was asked about a difficult situation in her career. She said "There was a point in my career where I found myself stuck in a bureaucratic web. I could not get anything done, and I was really unhappy. My manager at that time was trying to accelerate a critical project that I was leading. He decided to make management changes – and create virtual teams. I think he did that because it was the current trend to do so. I also had the sense that he wanted to make our project seem bigger than it really was. But, it was not very effective. We ended up having four managers for 15 engineers. This caused a lot of confusion and slowed things down. I was in a maze of constant negotiations and spinning my wheels. I finally left and found another job. Now I am in an environment with much less bureaucracy. I feel like I am trusted, valued and can make a difference. I am all for collaboration and virtual teams, but it has to make sense and be practical. At the end of the day, people need to feel like they can make a difference and get things done."

Example: Too many Cooks

NView is a project which aims to build the next generation platform. Its goal was to offer substantially improved performance, and scale as well as ease application integration and deployment. NView was originally a small project of about five engineers, headed by Carla. NView had started as a skunk-works project in Carla's team. She saw the potential and sold the idea to her VP, Randy. This allowed Carla to expand the project to about eight engineers and accelerate the development of some key features. Her goal was to achieve first release in nine months. Things were humming along, until Randy decided to "help".

Randy saw tremendous potential in NView and thought this could be the big win for his entire organization. However, he felt it was too big to be left up to just Carla. It would be better if he had a team of experienced managers working on NView – that would clearly set it up for success. Randy also thought this was the perfect opportunity to align with the current business trend of setting up collaborative virtual teams. This would give the project the importance that it needed. Having it just under Carla seemed to somehow play down the value.

So, Randy brought in Brad, Larry and George... three more managers and 7 more engineers to help accelerate the program. With this, Randy felt he could organize NView – which he viewed as a large, important and complex project – for maximum success. Brad had previous experience in building a similar solution. Randy thought Carla could leverage his work. Larry had a strong reputation for delivering complex projects, so Randy wanted him on the team. And now that there were four managers to coordinate, Randy hired George as a program manager for the team.

Soon, Carla found herself immersed in intense discussions with Larry, Brad and George about the merits of her project, why she cannot really leverage Brad's work and debating the roadmap and timeline. Her senior engineers were also pulled in to present status, technical overviews and discuss the merits of the planned features. There was much debate and revisiting decisions on how things "should really be done".

Carla and her team became very frustrated. She felt neither Brad, nor Larry had a clue about the technology or the vision. Carla felt they were big time wasters. She spent much of her time fending them off and avoiding their meetings. The once "go get 'em" momentum of Carla's team slowed to a crawl. Morale suffered, there was lots of gossiping and Carla's sour mood rubbed off on the team. Some of the leads started to look for other opportunities. This was definitely a case of "too many cooks in the kitchen". There were four managers and 15 engineers, which did not make sense. Despite the managers' efforts to compress Carla's schedule and add engineers to the project, the schedule actually expanded to 18 months. This is because the bureaucracy simply drove off some of the lead engineers. There was a huge productivity hit due to the added management overhead.

When the 18 month forecast was presented to Randy, he had a fit. How could this happen, after all the help he had provided to the project? Randy set out to find the cause behind the project slip. There was nothing documented that indicated the project slip was due to bureaucracy. The program meeting minutes focused on the various discussions that had transpired: status from Carla's team, a debate on how to pull things in, technical reviews, questioning how to leverage Brad's earlier work, etc. All this seemed normal … what was Randy missing?

Randy held discussions with each of the managers. What he learned is that Carla did not really view this additional set of managers as help. From her perspective, she felt that Randy did not trust her and that is why he added additional management. Besides, Carla was hoping to do well enough on this project that she could be promoted. With Larry and Brad in the picture, Carla felt she was not being considered for advancement. Carla informed Randy that she felt disempowered, and that the other managers actually slowed things down. The other managers viewed Carla as being territorial and difficult to work with.

Randy's real goals were to ensure the success of NView by bringing in more experienced managers into the project and use it as an opportunity to experiment with collaborative teams. Unfortunately, Randy's execution was muddled: he ended up building a twisted and ineffective leadership web. He took a good concept and implemented it as a bureaucracy which slowed things down considerably. There were far too many managers for the number of engineers. There was no need for such complexity for this project. The help that Randy meant to provide actually caused mistrust, morale issues, attritions and project slowdown. From Carla's perspective, it looked like Randy did not trust her and that he certainly was not interested in growing her career. The spirit had been sapped from the core software team and things slowed to a crawl.

Worse still, Randy had created a bureaucratic culture. To turn it around, he would need to slim down his team and get them focused again. Perhaps, he should let Carla go, since she seems to be the trouble maker? In reality, this made no sense. Carla was the star performer and the creative force of the program. However, everyone else found it difficult to work with Carla. She was viewed as a control freak. He decided to let her go. When that happened, there was also an exodus of the best engineers.

Randy tried to keep the program going but it eventually died. The other managers lacked the passion and vision that Carla possessed. The best engineers had left. The team was not able to execute effectively. After 1 year, four managers, and 15 engineers, the entire program folded. It was a failed experiment which cost the company a lot of time, money and valuable engineers.

Bureaucracy is like Butter

You need to use it sparingly!

The above example clearly illustrates how adding more management bandwidth may lead to more bureaucracy and slow things down. In addition, the bureaucracy has a compounding effect. To coordinate across the groups, another layer of managers is needed – program managers. They in turn create processes to manage status, metrics and transfer of data across groups. This creates a sub-culture of reporting and status collection to facilitate the decision making by the management. The more managers, the more data is needed to make decisions, the more meetings are needed to discuss issues and the longer it takes to make plans and execute. Another point to note in the story is that when things do go wrong, it is often much harder to figure out what went wrong and how to turn things around.

There is no status report that says "there were too many managers making decisions". The clues to look for are endless debates without reaching consensus and agreement; teamwork issues; attrition; execution slowdown; diminished excitement. The other very basic clue is to count the number of managers and the number engineers on a project. If the ratio is anything less than optimal (for example, between seven to ten engineers per manager), you need to watch for spirit-sapping bureaucracy and heavy politics that get in the way of doing good work. The larger the project, the more apt it is to fail and the longer it will take to figure out what went wrong and how to turn things around. The truth is that much harder to discover and analyze. However, we are not advocating anarchy! As we have seen earlier, good management is essential to good engineering. However, it is important to have the right balance. Too much management overhead in a software engineering organization slows down the iterative process and saps positive energy and creativity – all critical ingredients to happy, productive engineers.

The leadership hierarchy and density of an organization is one of the key catalysts for shaping engineering culture in an organization. To keep things nimble and light, managers should strive for a flat organizational structure, with straightforward project ownerships where possible. Collaborative virtual teams are generally preferred when working across distinct functional areas or across large numbers of engineers that need additional management guidance. Over-engineering the collaborative framework for small teams (such as in Carla's case) can hamper team work and slow things down. A light leadership web is a strong web.

SUMMARY LEADERSHIP ECOSYSTEM

This chapter described many stories that were leadership failures, and through them we have gained greater insight into the success factors for creating a vibrant leadership ecosystem.

The key success factors are:

- Hiring and retaining strong engineering managers
- Active executive engagement
- Sponsoring the engineering managers
- Fostering peer networks
- Minimizing bureaucracy

Focusing on these success factors will result in greater collaboration, effective decision making and a powerful leadership ecosystem. This is the foundation for enabling a strong culture and the success of your software team.

Organizational success stems from the strength of its leadership web. It forms the foundation for your culture and is a huge factor in the fueling the productivity of your teams.

At this point, take a moment to reflect on your leadership ecosystem. Have you done everything possible to ensure its success?

YOUR LEADERSHIP SUCCESS FACTORS

Here is a summary of the leadership success factors that you can use as a checklist in your organization:

Organization Success Factors	Your organization
Nurturing Leadership	
- Engineering manager traits	
- Technical competence	
- Focus and drive	
- Wins team mindshare	
- Active team management	
- Tuned into the team's mood	
- Excellent communications	
- Effective operations	
- Leadership ecosystem	
- Sponsored managers and leads	
- Strong peer networks	
- Minimal bureaucracy	
Close knit community	
Software Soul	
People-focused operations	

Section 3

Community

The Cultural Epicenter

Never doubt that a small group of committed people can change the world. Indeed it is the only thing that ever has – Margaret Mead

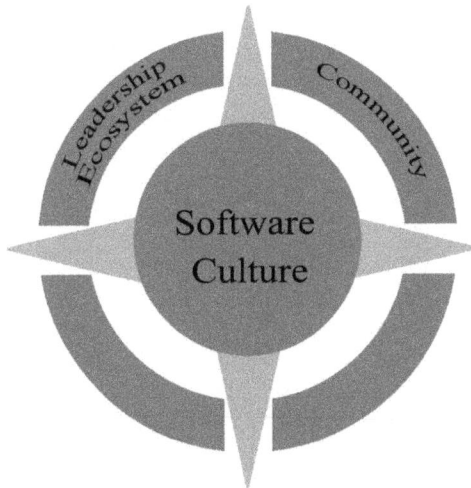

CULTURAL PILLARS
BUILDING GREAT TEAMS

We all know of teams that work well. What is their secret?

Technical skills are the foundation of any software engineering team. However, there are many teams with good engineers that simply flounder and are not able to produce very much. The good teams are able to conquer a myriad of challenges, seem very positive about their future, are fun to work with, and generally get things done. The dysfunctional teams have problems that impact end products through missed deliveries, poor quality and high numbers of customer issues. When we look a bit deeper, beyond the metrics, we see such teams quite often feel victimized, not in control of their destiny, and mired in distrust and apathy. What is even more interesting is that the technical capacities of the engineers in strong and dysfunctional teams are quite often comparable: something else as equally fundamental is critical to make teams work. That secret ingredient is the team culture.

Great teams have great culture that shapes the behavior of individuals and motivates the team to higher levels of excellence. Culture unleashes a sense of belonging to something big and important and can channel the team energy into something invincible – which is quite often what is needed to tackle the difficult problems that inevitably crop up during normal software engineering.

Some of the factors that shape team culture and dynamics are very unique to software engineering. For the most part, engineers are introverts, highly intellectual and logical. They expect human relationships to also be logical and systematic. In addition, 90 percent of engineers think they are in the top 25% of performers. As a result, you have a community of high-ego over-achievers that expect human interactions to be as fair and as predictable as the algorithms in their computer programs. Needless to say, engineers generally struggle in situations where the nuances of human interactions come into play. This makes it particularly challenging to build strong engineering teams.

This section describes the factors that strongly influence software engineering team dynamics and how they shape the cultural foundation.

These *cultural pillars* are:

- Roles and Responsibilities
- Communications
- Geography & distribution
- Diversity
- Team Esteem
- Team rituals

These pillars are briefly summarized below.

Roles and Responsibilities

When each person in the team has clearly-defined roles and responsibilities, it is much easier to establish clear accountability, cooperation, and striving toward common goals.

Communications

The power of human interaction and feeling like part of a community is powerful. It is far more powerful than any technology we have yet created!

Technology teams gravitate towards the latest gadgets, including communications gadgets. Balancing virtual communications with in-person communications is vital to creating a strong sense of community, establishing trust and accelerating the speed of engineering iteration.

Geography and Distribution

Physical Setup

The physical arrangement of a team is so fundamental that it is often overlooked. After all, there are many forms of technological communication that enable us to overcome the limitations of physical separation. There are times when a virtual setup suffices and other times when it is absolutely critical to have physical proximity to enable collaboration and boost productivity.

Multi-site, offshore teams

Offshore software development is a fact of life in our current business world. Going into it with clear business objectives and reward structures is critical to success. It is imperative to create a strategy that takes the long term view into account, review the effectiveness of the arrangement regularly, and be realistic about business expectations.

Diversity

Diversity fuels innovation and accelerates problem solving. There are different kinds of diversity: gender, ethnicity and skills. Ultimately, software engineering is about creativity. Having a diverse team of competent individuals boosts diversity of thought – a vital ingredient in any engineering team.

Team Esteem

The totality of the self-esteem within a team, combined with the team self-image, is a huge factor in team dynamics. A strong team-esteem fuels higher energy and productivity. When teams feel important, and know that their work has business impact, they will naturally strive to reach higher standards of performance. A team with strong team-esteem is positive, confident and invincible.

Team Rituals

Team habits of working and playing together day-to-day provides the fuel for the big battles. Strong teams get even stronger during challenging times. And the weak ones will wither even during normal operation. So, weave fun and meaningful rituals into the team cultural fabric. This is the web that will hold the team together when times get tough.

The next few sections will delve into each of these pillars in more detail and describe their impact on your business.

ROLES AND RESPONSIBILITIES

"Good fences make good neighbors" – said Robert Frost. Such is the case in any community, including an engineering community. It is important to have clear roles and responsibilities and boundaries so that everyone can work effectively together. We came across several teams where the senior leader had basically abdicated his responsibility to designate clear roles and responsibilities under the guise of "enabling collaboration". At the other end of the spectrum, we also saw cases where there was a rigid organizational framework – which fostered silos and limited collaboration.

Clearly defining the roles and responsibilities has a significant impact on the team harmony, trust and effectiveness. We saw many groups where lack of clear roles and responsibilities caused duplication of work, diminished accountability, slowed down decision making and eroded trust. Most notably, we saw examples in which a muddled state of affairs was the norm and the teams had been working in that mode for months and sometimes years. It seems that it is easier to disguise such confusion under the umbrella of "the project is just too large and complex" or "the team has to learn to collaborate" or even "I am too busy" rather than the senior leader stepping in to orchestrate the team into a collaborative framework and setting in place clear roles and responsibilities. Confusion over responsibilities can lead to costly missteps and significantly reduced team productivity; more importantly, it erodes the very foundation of the culture by diminishing trust, teamwork and morale. It is imperative for the senior leaders in the organization (VP, director and senior manager) to take charge and orchestrate the roles and responsibilities framework.

Let's look a couple of examples where roles and responsibilities were unclear and how this impacted the business.

> This story was inspired by an interview with Bill, who discussed a challenging situation where he had to leave a job due to confusion over his role. Bill said "I joined the company and Gord's team because I was offered an expanded role of doing more than just software development. I was really excited about being given the chance to dabble in some vendor management, and in fact I had turned down other offers. After a few months, Gord changed my role in the group without even talking to me. I became a standard software development manager again. I was really upset, and I decided to move on. Luckily, there are still lots of good opportunities out there".

Example – Gord: Ready, Fire, Aim

Gord was a director responsible for deploying several new applications on a brand new platform. He had three engineering managers, Bill, May and Joe, each charged with developing various applications. The three managers had gone through several discussions to parcel out the various projects among themselves. The development managers were particularly excited because they were also being tasked with additional responsibilities – such as marketing and engaging with vendors at trade shows. This added responsibility gave them each a new growth opportunity and it was one of the reasons that both Bill and May had joined the team. This was not just another development team; they could experience the full breadth of marketing, product development and deployment.

One day, out of the blue, Gord introduced a new manager to the team – John. John was hired by Gord to be the vendor management lead. This was disconcerting to all the development managers. Part of their charter, and the part they were most excited about, was being taken away and handed over to John. Gord had not discussed John's role and responsibilities with any of the development managers before hiring him. They were not sure how John would fit in. Everyone speculated that Gord wanted another manager under him to round out his portfolio. After all, Gord's peers who were moving up had bigger charters than Gord. The move also made it clear that Gord really did not care about growing the careers of his existing managers or asking for their inputs about the organization.

The trust between Gord and his management team was broken. The managers were unhappy and plodded through the next few months. Many times, John duplicated the efforts already underway in the development teams, and caused confusion with the user community – which was already dealing with May, Bill and Joe as the interfaces into the organization. The managers tried to get things done as much as possible without John's "help" – but, Gord called them on it and said they were not collaborating. This was a no-win situation. Finally, Bill and May just left the team altogether to seek other opportunities. After all, this was not the role they had signed up for and they did not feel they could trust Gord any longer to make good business decisions, or set them up for success in their careers.

Lessons from Gord's Story

This story illustrates the importance of establishing clear roles and responsibilities within an organization. Being clear on why a new role is being created, how it meets business needs and how it ties into existing roles in the group is a critical part of maintaining trust, and building a collaborative and cohesive team. Engineering managers expect to be consulted about upcoming organizational changes. These are not managers that should just 'be told' how things will change in the team. A big part of the engineering culture is collaboration – where there is at least some level of consultation and dialogue before implementation of organizational changes. Acting single-handedly like Gord can break trust and crumble the passion and drive that are so critical in engineering. Ultimately, lack of clarity around roles can lead to duplication of effort, loss of productivity, attrition of key talent and seriously jeopardize business goals.

Why would Gord not set clear roles and responsibilities? Many times, we heard about managers that avoid direct discussion of roles and responsibilities, organizational effectiveness and upcoming plans with their direct staff. Engineers and engineering leaders expect to be included in key decision making. Taking an authoritarian approach is a sure-fire way to alienate your staff – even if the changes are beneficial in the long term. Creating roles that infringe on existing charters is another sure fire way to cause mistrust and erode the positive energy in the team. The "old school" model of an authoritarian management hierarchy simply does not work in the engineering world.

The following story discusses a trait of some engineering managers: that of being too nice to set boundaries, and letting teams do whatever they want. This story was recounted to us by George, when asked to talk about a time when he learned a valuable lesson. George said "An important lesson I learned is that managers need to set rules and boundaries – and most importantly, they need to make timely decisions. I once worked for a really nice guy, Mike. However, he did not like to make difficult decisions and mostly avoided any kind of conflict. That made it very difficult for all of us – because, like any team, we had conflicts from time to time – and we looked to Mike to guide us through to a reasonable resolution. However, he was often missing in action and just avoided any kind of confrontation. And, that led our team into some standstills – which made us all look bad and really impacted our business. Mike eventually left. The new director was left with a messy situation and had to make some tough calls. I did not necessarily like all the decisions, but I respected him for making them. That made big difference. Let me give you an example of what happened and you will see what I mean".

Example: Mike the Marshmallow

This story is about Mike, a director of engineering with a staff of four managers. Mike is known as a nice guy. He is pleasant to work for, and takes care of his team. The only problem was that Mike's team seemed to do whatever they felt like and, as a result, there were duplicate responsibilities and many missed deliverables. In a nutshell, the team was highly ineffective.

A classic story that was told to us is about two of Mike's managers: George and Gary – both of whom were responsible for the same functional area, CBot. George and Gary each had about 10 engineers – so, there were a total of 20 engineers working on CBot. CBot was core to the company's business, and it was critical to have 7x24 support – and that was the initial justification of having duplicate teams, each in different parts of the world. However, CBot was constantly in trouble: missing deadlines on deliverables, creating customer escalations, and it was generally known as a poor product. How could this be, even with two engineering teams focused on one area?

A closer examination and discussions with Gary and George were revealing of the reasons. Each manager felt that they had no control over CBot and blamed the other team for the problems. George said his engineering team worked harder and gave a rundown of the features they had developed. Gary said the same thing. One thing neither said was how much care they took to answer customer issues, address the bug backlog or deal with rewriting code to improve maintainability. It was clear both George and Gary were after the glory of just developing new features and neither one had interest in ensuring a stable, and reliable product. When things failed, they simply blamed the other team.

Mike did not deal with this dual ownership. Instead, he played the friendly boss and portrayed the area as being so troubled that only two engineering teams could do it justice. In reality, Mike did not have the basic people skills to set boundaries and define clear roles for his organization. It was much easier to just let the team do what they wanted: he did not want to be viewed as a bad guy. Eventually, things got so bad that Mike was fired.

The new manager split responsibilities between Gary and George. Once their accountability was clarified, each of them stepped up and drove dramatic improvements in their respective areas. CBot thrived under Gary's leadership; George took on a new area. Both were happier, the teams were more productive and the business was more profitable. The magical energy had indeed been unleashed through a clarification of roles and responsibilities.

Clarify Roles, Get Mindshare, Now Go

So, somewhere between being authoritarian like Gord and disengaged like Mike lies a middle ground. People leadership in engineering requires the ability to set in place a roles and responsibilities framework that all parties believe in, trust and can ultimately thrive in. This requires having a dialogue with each individual to understand what makes them tick, what their interests are, and weaving that into the overall community goals. Simply assigning roles, based on business need, is required from time to time. But, it should be done on an exception basis and always in conjunction with individual goals. Obviously, some give and take will be needed to reach agreement.

Engineers and engineering managers are finicky when it comes to deciding to work on something. Many of them work because they want to make a difference and be valued – not just collect a paycheck. By understanding their motivations and interests, you can tap into their inner energy and set up each individual for success.

For example, if Gord had held discussions with his managers, he would have understood that having a broad charter was an important reason why they chose to work in his group. This could have made a big difference in the organizational structure and ultimately in the success of his business.

Similarly, Mike could have held discussions with his managers about their needs and interests. He would have received feedback about the ineffective nature of the dual ownership model. He would have understood the need for his managers to have clear ownership and accountability. This would have led to creating a more effective organization sooner and mitigated the business losses.

Without an explicit understanding of who is responsible for what, each person will strive to do what they *think* is expected of them, and this inevitably leads to duplicate efforts, sluggish execution, missed deliveries and poor support.

The roles and responsibility framework is the pillar that orchestrates the team in to a concerted mode of operation. It is a vital part of building a harmonious, functional software community.

COMMUNICATIONS

While engineers have the reputation of being nerdy and anti-trendy, they are very much "techno fashionistas": most of them are very aware of trends in their industry and adopt the latest gadgets. The latest trend is an exponential increase in communications. From the internet, to email, to cell phones, it is now possible to be virtually connected to anyone at anytime. The engineering community has embraced these communications technologies to significantly improve its effectiveness.

However, it also brings some unique challenges – especially when such technology is used to circumvent human contact and open communications. A very typical scenario is illustrated by the following story.

This story was recounted to us by Susan, when asked to talk about the challenges of managing engineers. She said "Email is a blessing and a curse. I find that many engineers would rather send email than talk to each other. Most engineers think efficiency is more important than building relationships – so email is their preferred communications. But, using email in the wrong situations can actually cause harm. One team I managed was really difficult because the most senior engineer dealt with most of his communications by email – and he was really harsh. This created a cloud of negativity in the group, and the team could not work well together. So, I finally set some rules to bring people together face to face as much as possible. It took a while, but this made a huge difference. People started trusting each other a lot more and problems were solved a lot faster. Email is great – but, it really can't replace the human touch. After all, engineers are people too".

Example: Email Warfare

Susan, a manager of a small software engineering team told us about a situation where she found several of her engineers engaged in an "email war of words".

The scenario is a code review being conducted by a technical lead in the team. The mails went something like this. The tech lead wrote "Are you kidding? You've completely missed the point. This is a pretty simple problem and you have not dug into this enough. What you have is a hack. I will not approve this in its current state...." In response, the engineer receiving the comments fired an email back with "Well, I don't have time to keep revising this. I have been asked to fix just a specific problem, and that is what I am doing. I don't think this is a hack. Do you think you can do better? In fact, why don't you just take over and finish it?" Needless to say, things deteriorated from there and it took a long time to reach consensus.

Susan was aware of many such cases in her group – where the engineers used email to fight with each other and demonstrate their technical superiority – rather than meeting in person and using personal influence to talk things through. Sometimes, things deteriorated to the point where the engineers would escalate the war into an all out series of email flames. There just was not much human and emotional collateral at stake with email – so, it was easy to be nasty.

So, Susan tried a different tack and asked that any discussion that takes more than three email volleys be conducted in person. When the engineers got into one room to solve a problem, they were almost always awkward, hiding behind their laptops and less prone to attack their peers. The spoken words took longer to materialize than emails – but, that was a good thing because when the words did come out, they were far milder and less confrontational than email. Susan said, "Once engineers got into the habit of talking to their peers face to face, they got along better because they were looking at someone while talking – and it was much harder to be hostile. In turn, the problems were solved faster, and the team became a lot stronger".

It turns out that engineers would be more likely to engage in a negative exchange if they had never met or rarely meet the person within their virtual world. Left to their own devices however, engineers preferred working in the virtual world to such an extent that quite often they would debate on email rather than meeting engineers sitting within a 10 minute radius. The anonymity of the email medium had given them a crutch for not dealing with the nuances of human relations and building healthy peer relationships.

Similarly, teleconferences and wikis are staples of engineering business life and should be used to complement, not entirely replace, face to face contact between team members.

An interesting example of this was the case of Casey, a very capable but extremely introverted engineer. This story was told to us by Scott, when asked to talk about some insights into managing engineers. He said "It is really important to build good relationships between your engineers. Without that, it is hard to get things done. A big part of that is making sure you have enough face time. Team meetings are important to have in person because when you see someone you interact with them completely differently than if you just dealt with them on the phone. I once had a very difficult engineer – Casey – who was brilliant, but a complete introvert. Casey couldn't communicate even if her soul depended on it! She rarely interacted with the team. Because she was critical to our success, I spent a lot of time coaching her and tried to shape her behavior. It took a long time. Shaping engineers is definitely harder than shaping computer programs. But, I was able to get her to attend team meetings in person and actually interact. That made a huge difference to the overall team productivity – because people were able to talk with Casey so much more easily."

Example: Hiding in the Virtual World

Scott had taken over as manager of an engineering group and started holding weekly staff meetings.

Scott noticed that Casey, one of the brightest engineers on the team, would dial in via teleconference, did not participate and was essentially missing in action. Scott knew the previous manager had let this slide. After all, Casey was irreplaceable and she did great work. But Scott wanted to build a high energy team, and knew that if he did nothing about Casey's behavior, the rest of the team would view it as his implicit acceptance of bad behaviors in the group. After all, Casey was a senior engineer and her behavior influenced the other team members.

Scott set in place and communicated a new policy: show up in person to the staff meeting. Casey consistently failed to show up. So, Scott tried a different tack. At the sixth staff meeting, Scott said "I really appreciate everyone making an effort to show up in person to our staff meeting. It makes a big difference to our team spirit and what we can achieve". Scott continued "Casey, we would like you to join us. It will make a difference". Casey hung up on the teleconference. The room was quiet and Scott felt the stares of the engineers – somewhat accusing him of making Casey angry. However, what happened next was truly surprising. Casey showed up at the staff meeting in person. Scott said, "Thank you Casey. That was fast". To which she said "No problem. I was just dialed in from my cube". Her office cube was 20 feet from the conference room. Scott just smiled and continued.

Over the next few weeks, Scott able to build more discussion into the staff meeting and even draw Casey out of her shell. Having Casey engaged in the team enabled the team to get a deeper technical knowledge of areas she was familiar with, and the other engineers felt more comfortable asking her questions and were able to achieve more as a team by bringing everyone into the live community.

Live Communications Shape Teams

The power of in-person human interaction and being part of a live-community is far more powerful than any technology we have yet created. It is an essential ingredient in building strong teams.

Setting up a communications framework that brings the engineering team into regular contact makes a big difference. It is just that much harder to flame someone when you are talking to them face to face. You need to look someone in the eye and understand their point of view, adjust your tone of voice, and try to get along. That makes all the difference in building trust and enabling open, respectful communications. This in turn enables more information sharing, which is vital to problem solving and innovation.

Today's technologies, such as video conferencing, can help with this objective and should be used to connect engineers whenever in-person communications are not possible. However, budgets should be allocated such that the engineering team can meet regularly in person to build relationships.

Enabling in-person communications is a key pillar to improving productivity, and can make the difference between a successful and a failed software project – which has a huge impact on the bottom line.

GEOGRAPHY

Geography plays a huge role in culture. Communities that live together use a common language, have common values and rituals. Everyone in the geographic community adopts certain cultural traits that allow them to work together and succeed in their environment.

Imagine if that same community is distributed across different geographical zones and asked to work together on common goals. It will be challenging to say the least. Everything from basics such as values and knowledge, to accepted rituals, to simply working together becomes more difficult. Add different time zones into this mix and you have the challenges faced by many software teams today.

Software engineering teams that need to collaborate on a daily basis work more effectively when they are geographically collocated. Yet, when projects are created, this basic fact is often overlooked or viewed as something that can be circumvented using communication technologies. As a result, project teams are often distributed across several buildings, time zones and geographies. Teams that never meet in person, teams that need to work that much harder to articulate common goals, track dependencies, solve problems – and teams that simply need to overcome more obstacles to get a high quality product shipped out on time. This extra work is a drain on engineering teams. Since we quite often don't allocate extra time for all the added coordination – this makes it more likely that delivery schedules will be missed.

Distributed teams are an inevitable part of software engineering. Today's business reality demands that the best engineers be leveraged for a project – no matter where they are physically located. How the project is partitioned, and how the team is actually organized, plays a big role in whether the project succeeds or fails. It is important to understand the motivations for creating a distributed team, and how to set it up for success.

Let's examine different aspects of how geographical challenges impact software teams and how one can create successful teams in a single-site environment and a multi-site environment.

Single Site Environment

Many people we interviewed indicated that basic things like physical location and office layouts are critical factors in making teams happy and productive. However, they cited being part of initiatives that invest in multi-million dollar projects to drive productivity, but paid little attention to how the team is physically arranged. This can really boomerang on the team effectiveness and project success. The following example illustrates the importance of physical location and its role in enabling stronger team dynamics.

This story was told by Alice, when asked to talk about some of the factors in improving engineering productivity. She said "I continue to be amazed at how engineering organizations spend lots of effort on improving productivity – but, fail to look at the basics. Having your engineers in one physical area is critical for building teamwork. It makes a huge impact on improving productivity. I would like to see a model where team members that need to interact frequently are collocated for the project duration. However, I usually get a lot of push back from my management when I suggest this. I get the sense they somehow don't want to acknowledge this basic human need. They seem to be more open to bringing in technology to circumvent communications challenges. I know that office moves cost money but I think it is worth it when you consider the benefits."

Example: Getting Closer, Working Better

A team was formed under Alice to head up a brand new initiative, project X. Project X had the potential to generate $100 million in the first year – should the team be able to deliver a viable product. There was huge pressure on Alice to prototype Project X quickly, obtain client feedback and achieve a production release. Alice was thrilled to be leading the project and felt she had the management sponsorship to make this succeed.

There were some immediate glaring problems that she needed to address however. The engineers in her team were scattered across multiple floors, and different buildings on the campus. The engineers were new to the technology, and had not worked with each other before. Alice knew this would make it very difficult for them to get their jobs done. More than anything, she needed a trusting, reliable and motivated team to drive this project. She knew from experience that even the best planned software projects had many problems. If the team did not have trust and mutual respect, these technical problems will take longer to surface and longer to fix – and ultimately delay the project.

Alice approached her management and asked that the team be collocated in an area close to each other with regular access to a conference room where the engineers can work together and discuss ideas. Her management was initially not open to this. They suggested that she leverage various web 2.0 technologies, such as wikis, chats, and shared workspaces to bring the team together. They also offered the services of a program manager to coordinate the activities of the engineers and thereby improve communications.

Alice agreed with her management that wikis, emails and teleconferences were useful tools, and her plan was to leverage them for communications between her team and other product teams with whom they would need monthly integration discussions. But her engineers needed to work closely together every day and she felt that a stronger team could be built faster if the team had "face time" to build trusting relationships. She also knew that engineers were especially averse to dealing with the "people stuff" that would be needed to enable teamwork and speedy problem solving. Alice insisted that collocation of her own team would result in accelerated project execution.

The management's main concerns with the proposal were it would cost hundreds of dollars per engineer to collocate them, and that a precedent would set for other projects. Will everyone demand an arrangement like Alice's? Alice pointed out that the investment of a few thousand dollars for moving eight engineers was peanuts compared to the overall project cost (of $5 Million), and it would significantly accelerate their deliverables. Alice convinced her executives that the physical collocation of the team members would be critical to the project success.

The engineers were collocated shortly thereafter. To everyone's delight, the engineers built close relationships, ramped up very quickly, and were able to progress rapidly on their prototype. There was a positive air, and high energy that enabled the team to challenge each other to new heights of excellence and tackle the difficult problems quickly. Furthermore, the executives found that they had easy access to this team: they could just walk in to the engineering work area and ask for a quick update or discuss the latest technical challenges. This allowed the management to unblock issues quickly and keep the team moving. As a result, the prototype was built on time, and the team was able to showcase some cool features that were above and beyond what they had originally planned.

Balancing Live and Virtual Communities

In our high tech age, where there are many technologies to help us overcome the limitations of distance, there is a temptation to overlook physical organization altogether. We seem to be far more interested in emulating reality through technology than using what is natural and straightforward. Engineers being fascinated by technology also gravitate towards more anonymous, technological means of communications. This has its merits and its drawbacks.

In general, a collocated team is more effective for highly intense, fast paced projects that require daily interactions. Engineers can more easily tune into the nuances of the human network, build trust and form bonds – all of which are critical in problem solving and innovation. In a fast paced project, or a project where a team is being built for the long term, one needs to examine the immediate cost of moving teams versus the long term cost of missed deadlines, quality woes, and morale issues. Close proximity is critical to accelerating the bonds of a well functioning team.

There are definitely situations when virtual teams are practical. For example, if the project components are split at a macro level such that it does not require daily or weekly calls and technical negotiations, it is likely that infrequent discussions suffice. In these situations, there is no need for physical collocation. There are excellent advances in communications technology, such as web conferencing, that make it possible to have the as-need, less intensive, communications. In fact, this would be more cost effective in this scenario.

It all comes down to judgment. An engineering manager should be empowered to decide the physical configuration for their teams and determine whether a virtual team is practical versus one that is collocated. General guidelines are:

- Collocated team for highly intense projects requiring daily discussions or for teams that need to start up together on a complex engineering project
- Collocation not required when there are well defined boundaries of ownership, and interface points. That is, there is no need for daily communications.

Ideally, you would want an environment that is fluid to meet the ever-changing needs of teams as they work through various projects. It is understood that in reality things are not so simple. There is typically lots of red tape involved in moving people from A to B. In our age of high tech, and mobile communications, moving should be a snap. If managers could configure workspaces for their teams to suit project needs, the productivity gains would be tremendous. In the initial project planning, consideration of physical and virtual teams is an important aspect of setting up software teams and projects for success.

Multi Site Teams

With the proliferation of offshoring, it has become the norm to have multi-site, overseas software project teams. The engineering talent pool is huge in countries such as India and China. It is in our best interest to welcome such talent to North America as well as to leverage that talent pool for business success.

The level of success seems to very much be in the eye of the beholder. At the grassroots level, offshoring is deemed to not work by a majority of the people we spoke with. VPs and higher ranking individuals on the other hand, gave a much rosier picture. Why the discrepancy? One person that was interviewed said "It all comes down to relativity". Two observers of the same phenomenon experience it differently depending on their point of view. So it is with multi-site teams and offshore software projects.

Dave, a typical engineering manager, captured the sentiments of many when he said "My team is just tired of 7 AM and 10 PM calls multiple times a week. No one realizes the human cost of doing global business. There is no recognition of the fact it takes five times more effort to make a global, multi-site project work. Getting any normal software project to succeed is hard enough, without adding this additional twist. I am not just talking about my

North American team. I had several people quit in India because it was difficult for them to juggle early morning and late night calls".

So, why are offshore, multi-site teams created? What are the motivations? Is there any way to make them succeed or at least less painful? This is obviously a fact of life in the software world. On the surface at least, there appears to be a huge upside: the leverage of a large pool of highly talented engineers at low cost. Yet, it is obvious that it is a source of stress and energy drain. Knowing what works and what some of the pitfalls are can help set up a software team for greater success.

Let's explore this in a bit more detail.

Two reasons seem to crop up time and again when we ask about the motivations for offshore, multi-site team formations:

1. Cost
2. Strategy

Reason 1: Cost

Let's look at cost – since that is the most obvious reason and the one that is most often cited. Labor costs are significant in the US. Let's assume a Silicon Valley software engineer's loaded labor rate is $ 200K / year and that the loaded labor rate of an engineer in India is about $70K/year. That means we can get about three engineers in India for each North American engineer. That would imply three times the amount of productivity. This means by hiring three engineers overseas, a project team can potentially create three times the content, fix three times the bugs, and compress the timeline for a project significantly. The promise of more features, with better quality, faster, and at lower cost is just too good to resist. That is one of the main motivations for moving software development overseas: you get more for your money. Is that really true?

Let's have a closer look at the reality. Like many things in life, what looks too good to be true usually is.

> The illusion of cost savings was best captured in a discussion with Diane, a seasoned engineering manager. When asked to share her views on multi-site and offshore development, she said "First, let me say I am amazed at the global talent in software engineering. We absolutely need to leverage that talent to improve the software business. But, I think the way organizations go about setting up offshore teams often does not work. There is a difference in how success of such projects is viewed at the executive versus the grassroots levels. I just recently left a company because I found myself doing two jobs – one where I was driving an overseas tech transfer and another where I was starting new project. I was stretched thin, the team was frustrated and we had too much attrition. My counterpart in India had the same challenges. Our executives seemed to be more concerned with the optics of aligning with the offshore mantra rather than really engaging in the process. I felt there were many layers of delusion at play here. In reality, cost reductions take a while to materialize. I will say that even though the project was not successful, I built great friendships with my Indian colleagues. That is something I really treasure. Let me tell you the story and you will understand what I mean".

Example: Cut costs, move this overseas

Diane was recently asked to transfer her functional area to India to help reduce overall development and support costs of an existing product. Mohan was hired as the manager of the India team and he hired a staff of 10 engineers to mirror Diane's local team. The executives expected the India team to be up and running in four months and at that point Diane's team was to move on to a new program. Diane and one of her senior engineers made a trip to India to bootstrap the training. A couple of the engineers from India came back to North America to receive onsite training. So, after three months of aggressive training, things looked like they could finally get going. That is when the trouble all began.

Diane was all set to hand over the reins to Mohan. After all, she had to start ramping up her team on the new area. The India team however, experienced several problems. Mohan found it difficult retain top talent when the job at hand was essentially to take over legacy technology. Once the engineers learned this, they started leaving. After all, the market was hot and there were more exciting opportunities. The engineers that remained were more junior and required a lot of handholding.

There were calls with the North American team at 7 AM and again at 9 PM for months on end. Mohan made a recommendation to double the India staff in order to get the required productivity. It took a couple of months to fill all the positions. This time, he hired mainly junior engineers so that they would not be as put-off about inheriting a legacy product. The added headcount brought with it another set of challenges. Coordination was required between the engineers, their partner teams and clients in North America. Mohan was simply not able to scale. So, a North American program manager was brought to track deliverables, report status, and coordinate between Mohan's team and others.

In the meantime, four months had elapsed. According to the original plan, the new team was supposed to be on par with the Diane's old team by now. In reality, they were still ramping up and struggling with their deliverables. So, Diane's management asked her to continue helping Mohan's team. This meant she and some of her engineers ended up doing two jobs rather than focus their full efforts on the new project. The team was wearing thin. It seemed that they were doing all the work, and not getting any credit. It was very discouraging. Mohan tried to accelerate the learning curve in his team – but, some of the engineers complained about being over-worked and not receiving sufficient training. It seemed to be a no-win situation. Diane and Mohan both tried to flag these concerns to their management and seek guidance. However, their management put the blame on them, saying they must be flawed in their execution and that they had poor teamwork.

Soon, some of Diane's top engineers left. Diane decided to leave the company altogether. She did not feel set up for success and her health had started to deteriorate. Mohan decided to take another job where he would be responsible for creating the product strategy and roadmap. He really wanted to have more say in the business decisions – and not just follow orders from North America. This was far more exciting than dealing with a lengthy technology transfer.

The executive team was now left with two very troubled areas, and customer expectations that clearly could not be met for either the old or new product. What a mess! They estimated it will take another 6 months to put each functional area back on track.

How much did that really cost?

The main rationale for moving technology overseas is to reduce costs. Many at the grassroots told us that they think this is a myth. So, we decided to dig a bit deeper to understand what the full cost of this strategy would be.

Now, let's tally the approximate costs in the example above. The following assumptions are made in the cost calculations:

Note: these numbers are just for illustration. It is suggested to use this as a framework and plug in numbers for your offshore projects to get a more realistic insight into your costs.

$200K per head in North America

$70K per head in India

$20 million per year revenue for the legacy product

$30 million per year revenue for the new product

Original Cost	Cost of Diane & Mohan Project
Diane + 10 engineers	$ 2 million
Cost of Tech Transfer	
Mohan + 15 engineers	$ 1.1 million
Program Manager	$200 K
Cost of attritions	
India Attritions	$200K
North America Attritions	$800K
Other Costs	
Travel	$50K
Lost revenue opportunity due to 6 month slip	$10 million for legacy product + $15 million for new product
Total cost for Tech Transition	~ $5 million
Cost of lost revenues	~ $25 million
Total Cost	$ 30 million

In this case, the cost of business during tech transfer is much greater than the cost of having a single-site team. Any cost advantage will take time and patience. Some managers indicated a period of 2-3 years of close monitoring, extended stays, and knowledge transfers to fully establish an offshore team. During that time of transition, the cost is high. After that time, once equilibrium is established, costs can be brought down to some extent.

Costs at equilibrium (after 2-3 years):

Costs at Equilibrium (after 2-3 years)	
Mohan + 15 engineers	$1.1 million
Program manager	$200K
Total costs at equilibrium	$1.5 million

So, net effect is that there is some long term cost savings after the 2-3 year mark. But, there is an uphill battle to get to that point. Transferring technology overseas is not a simple task. The 2-3 year cost is high and can result in product delays, quality issues and employee and customer dissatisfaction. There are no silver-bullet short-term successes. A long-term strategy that takes into account a fuller picture is needed.

Reason 2: Strategy

The second reason often cited for offshoring is that it is strategic. The viewpoint here is that for a company to compete globally, it needs to have a global presence. That makes a lot of sense. In fact, in some countries, you are required to have an R&D presence to sell there. If this is the prime motivation, be clear about it and don't muddle it with costs. This is a fact of life for doing business in certain regions of the world. This does not really necessitate a multi-site, close-knit development team. For such scenarios, you would be better off creating a wholly contained charter for the offshore team and give them full ownership and accountability. There should be no prolonged period of technology transfer, hand holding and frequent interactions at the grassroots level.

The following is an example where a strategic decision was made to create an offshore team. This story was recounted to us by Janet, who is Director of engineering at a mid-sized company. We asked her to share a story about multi-site, offshore software engineering. She said "Well, I have tried different techniques over the years, and I must say I have had my share of failures. It is tough to make offshore teams and projects work well. However, I think I found a formula that can work – and that is to establish entire charters overseas. Last year, my company made a strategic decision to expand into the China market – with one of my products leading the way. To make inroads in China, you really need some R&D presence. However, I did not want to tie my core team down in a lot of bureaucracy and a complex web of cross-ocean interactions. I know this can be a big productivity killer. At the same time it was of strategic importance to our business to expand globally – we simply had to find a way to make it work. So this is what I did."

Example: Strategy and Global expansion

Janet was Director of Engineering at a mid-sized company. She led a very successful product line, and was highly regarded for her operational efficiency. The team had top talent and high productivity. She knew that offshoring would be critical to the global success of her business, but her past attempts had failed. She was now facing another opportunity and another set of challenges.

Her company wanted to expand into the China market. Janet's product line was being positioned as one of the crown jewels of this effort. The marketing team thought that they could easily win a 20% market share in China in the eighteen months. But, there was a catch. To have credibility and mindshare with the Chinese customers, the company needed to establish a local R&D presence.

Janet had done the "offshore experiment" enough times to know the mistakes to avoid. She decided to try something different this time. Her idea was to create a completely new charter in China, to augment the existing product line. The China team will develop a monitoring, diagnostics and reporting tool – as an adjunct to the existing product. She also decided to de-risk the venture by starting with something of lower technical complexity, and not on the critical path, so that she could gauge the capacity of the offshore team. Of course, retaining the high productivity level in her core North American team was critical. She could not afford to slow them down. She also wanted to emulate that success in her new China team. Janet felt that creating a fairly contained charter that did not require regular grassroots interactions was an important factor in setting up the teams for success.

Finally, Janet wanted to make sure her executive management chain understood the costs and benefits of this plan. She approached the discussions with the executives somewhat cautiously. Her experience was that they would yearn for a Lamborghini, but only be willing to pay for a Chevy. She had to bring them back to reality. She held several meetings with them to explain the costs required to bootstrap the effort successfully. She requested that one of her top managers, Wayne, transfer to China for one year to help establish the R&D team there. Janet wanted buy-in from the executives that this was a strategic decision – and not one purely driven by cost. Otherwise, she knew the plan would not succeed. Luckily, Janet was able to convince them of the merits and costs of establishing this strategic overseas presence. The fact that Janet was highly regarded and had the sponsorship of her management chain made a difference.

The China R&D presence was kicked off shortly after that by Janet and Wayne. Wayne hired top Chinese engineers and he was able to successfully deliver the product in the scheduled timeframe. The local team felt that they controlled their own destiny and were able to build an excellent product. Wayne not only delivered the product but had created a strong team – the nucleus of growing a strong R&D presence. Janet's North American team had almost no day-to-day involvement with the Chinese team. Wayne ran the show. Both teams were highly productive.

Janet knew from her previous efforts that the failure paths are many in creating offshore, multi-site teams. She had learned the hard way that there are no easy ways to cut costs. Taking a longer term, strategic view is more realistic. An upfront acceptance of costs, a strong dose of experience, pragmatism and patience are critical to make this successful.

Offshore Success Strategy Factors

There are definitely some key ingredients in enabling the success of offshore, multi-site teams. Some of the common factors that surfaced during our interviews are listed below.

- Offshore at the right organizational level

  The offshore effort is particularly challenging and one that requires influence at the executive level to succeed. For example, there are significant costs to consider as well as creating the right business strategy. It is best to have offshore teams report to someone at a high enough level in the organization that can make broad business decisions with a full acceptance of the costs, risks and rewards. Having teams of engineers report into lower levels in the organization is usually unsatisfying and unproductive for both the offshore and main office teams.

- Full ownership of self contained products or components

Offshore teams should have complete ownership of products, components or charters – with full accountability, risks and rewards. Teams that own entire charters feel empowered, valued and energized to make a difference. Contrast with offshore teams that are positioned as "helpers" where they just handle maintenance, or supplement projects from the mother ship: there is a lot less ownership, and commitment to the overall project.

Furthermore, the boundaries of ownership should be such that there are infrequent interactions across the ocean. Infrequent is about once a month or less. No one wants to be on weekly early morning/late night conference calls.

- Tech transfers versus starting a brand new product

There are pros and cons to each approach. Tech transfers are appealing because they open avenues for the experienced team in the main office to take on the next innovative project. However, tech transfers take considerable time and effort – and there is a human and financial cost to consider. It generally leads to more bureaucracy and around the clock conference calls. Starting a brand new product is very appealing since it reduces the need for a complex web of grassroots interactions, empowers the local team to drive their destiny and provides more growth opportunities for the offshore team. However, there is a significant start up cost in the new product scenario – especially if the offshore team does not yet have the expertise to drive the charter on its own.

- Establish success criteria and a "perpetual beta" mindset

We encourage you to think about the offshore strategy as being in a perpetual beta state. There are very few cases where it is working well – and there is ample opportunity for improvements. So, go in with the attitude that things will need to be improved continuously and you will need to identify and fix problems quickly. Similar to a software project, it is important to review the offshore setup regularly, debug any issues and quickly rectify problems. Lingering issues typically manifest themselves in discontented teams, poor quality and reduced customer satisfaction. Establishing clear criteria for product delivery, key metrics, frequently reviewing the data, and holding teams fully accountable is critical to success.

An exceptional global operational framework, with clear success criteria, is needed to manage the deliverables of multiple teams and monitor the effectiveness of the overall arrangement.

- International Leadership Exchange

Seeding an offshore team with leaders from the main office and having regular extended international assignments for personnel is crucial for creating and maintaining the right culture. This encompasses leaders at all levels – from executives to engineers. This will drive the exchange of best practices, values, and create consistent high standards for your engineering teams – no matter where they are located. This is a significant investment of time, effort and money. The payback is that offshore teams will share the same values and practices as the main office teams, and they will learn the ropes first-hand from more experienced people – the leaders - in the company. The teams in the main office will be more attuned to the special challenges of the offshore teams and adjust their operations. This needs to be an ongoing process to enable business in a global environment.

- The teams in the "mother ship" should still run fast

  One of the most critical success factors is being able to create offshore teams without crippling your teams in the main office. As we saw in the Diane and Mohan example, there are many cases where the team in the main office ends up doing double duty. They feel like they have to do two jobs: transfer the technology and start on a new project. They feel like they don't get credit for their work and are not fairly rewarded for this double duty.

  Decisions about the offshore project will influence the productivity of the main office team. Having the offshore team run with a self contained project will minimize disruption to the main office team. Alternately, setting up a special reward scheme to recognize the additional effort required to do the tech transfer might be another way to maintain morale and productivity.

Following these guidelines makes it more likely that all the teams in the multi-site environment will be successful. Teams are empowered, can strive for their goals relatively independently of each other and move a lot faster to achieve focused business objectives. It is purely driven by business ownership and accountability for meeting business targets.

Most importantly, the offshore decision is a strategic decision. There is significant upfront and ongoing cost to do this well. If you want a Lamborghini, then you need to be prepared to pay for it. If you are ready to invest, the benefits are also great in terms of a stronger global business.

Replay: The Diane and Mohan Story

Let's reconsider the example of Diane and Mohan. If Diane had completely transferred ownership and accountability to Mohan after four months, Mohan's team may very well have run into the same issues. However, the problem would have been more contained: the team impact and business impact would be localized to Mohan's team. Diane's team could continue on their projects and her team and business would not be impacted. The executives could also have designed a reward structure for Diane, Mohan and their teams such that there are incentives associated with meeting a four month technology transfer milestone. Subsequent rewards for the teams would be aligned with their usual business metrics and deliverables. Hence, we can speculate that Mohan would also be more motivated to turn things around quickly since he is on his own rather than having an easily accessible life-line. This would also help boost the morale of all the engineering teams involved. Engineers know they would be held to high levels of accountability and rewards and rise to the challenge.

Summary - Offshore Strategy

How an offshore strategy is executed can profoundly impact your engineering teams. The umbilical cord strategy, with world-wide intensive collaborative interactions is a drain on most teams. No one wants to work around the clock. No one wants to engage in prolonged, painful technology transfers and not be fairly rewarded. The strategy also cannot be based on visions of "software imperialism" where one is trying to establish a global empire for selfish reasons. This will surely backfire.

Teams need to have clear charters, and accountability for their areas. A successful strategy must have this as an end goal. A successful execution must strive to reach this end goal quickly, with clear milestones and rewards. The cost of lingering in a transition period is simply too high – emotionally and financially.

The Software Village

Offshore software development is a fact of life in our current business world. Going into it with clear business objectives, expectations, and reward structures is critical to make it work. The obvious cost benefits may not necessarily translate to profitability in the short term. There is transition period of several years to reap the rewards. During the transition, the financial and human costs to a team are often high. It is imperative to create a strategy that takes this long term view into account and design a reward structure that is commensurate with the monumental efforts required to make an offshore strategy succeed.

For single-site projects, managers should be empowered to weigh the costs versus benefits of collocating their engineers. For highly intense, interactive projects, physical proximity of the whole team can significantly boost productivity by acceleration the pace of engineering iterations.

Virtual teams are effective when there are relatively infrequent interactions among the team members. There are great advances in technology that make this a very viable option in this case. The need for regular human interactions remains high in collaborative software projects. This builds trust and bonds the engineering team together – which is critical to the overall happiness and productivity of the team. A pragmatic balance of virtual and physically collocated teams based on project boundaries and frequency of interaction can significantly boost business profitability.

DIVERSITY

Engineering vitality is driven by ideas. You need a team that is capable of generating new ideas as well as implementing those ideas and taking them to fruition. A team that is comprised of individuals from diverse backgrounds is more likely to create innovative ideas, and be more adept at solving problems. Why? Diverse backgrounds bring together different experiences, different skills, and different problem solving approaches. This in turn boosts innovation, and accelerates problem solving.

Diversity often implies gender and ethnic diversity. Because gender and culture play a powerful role in our behavior, these factors are strong influencers of diverse thinking. However, skills diversity is also critical. This section will consider these three different types of diversity and how they impact the team dynamics, organization and diversity of thought.

As a prelude to this section, let it be stated that this section may be seen as controversial. It is not meant to offend, but to educate people on the reality that exists in software engineering. I would also like to point out that I am a female of Indian heritage, raised in a multi-ethnic environment. I have the deepest regard for diversity. Yet, some of what is said here is difficult – it is kind of like sharing a family secret. So, take a deep breath and read on….

Mars and Venus – Gender Diversity

Software engineering is a male-dominated profession. It is a well known fact that men and women think and act differently. If diversity is essential to creativity and problem solving, and women can provide that diversity, there would seem to be a solid business case to seek out strong women for their engineering teams. This is difficult to achieve for a couple of reasons. First, women comprise at most 20% of software engineering teams. Many of them enter the company with equal technical qualifications, but later find themselves relegated to support and project management roles. The engineering managers themselves tend to choose in their own image – meaning they tend to trust those that think, look, and act like themselves. This is human nature. Since most engineering managers are men, this in effect makes it less likely for women to be included in hot technical projects or be appointed engineering leads. I once read that the best way for a woman to get ahead in engineering is to appear weak and non-threatening. Apparently, male engineers have a problem dealing with strong female engineers. It is also true that because women are generally thought of as weak, they are not considered strong enough to pursue engineering careers – and certainly not engineering leadership.

This duality of how women are perceived and what women need to do to get ahead in engineering, almost certainly sets them up for failure. Bottom line is that to leverage the potential of your female engineers, management needs to help seed changes. This is just good business sense. You will fully leverage the technical potential in your team and enable greater creativity and innovation. Once the seeds are there and *nurtured*, it sets an example for others to follow. It also sets up a great reputation for your team as being open, merit-based and a great place to work.

Implementing gender diversity can give you a business edge. Recent studies such as "The Business Case for Gender Diversity" by Caroline Simard [4] of the Anita Borg institute clearly make that case.

How can an engineering leader promote diversity? First, when forming engineering teams, and appointing leadership roles, look beyond your comfort zone. See who brings in strong technical skills and a diverse background. As a leader, you need to be comfortable having people on your team who think, act and look different from you. Trial them out as part of a team, see what the results are. If the results look good, and the leader has made a difference, see how you can grow that person or promote them. Having diversity in the leadership team has a double benefit: the leader brings in new thinking, and they will attract other people of diverse backgrounds into your organization.

Here is a story of how seeding diversity led to a huge difference in the business profitability and success of a team. This story is from my personal experience of being hired into an engineering management role for a struggling team.

Example – Diversity Sparks Turnaround

A few years ago, I accepted a position as the engineering manager for a struggling team. It had been a troubled area for many years and needed to be re-energized into action. The area had a significant impact to the business and the fact that it was failing had huge ramifications. The manager hired me because I was one of the few people willing to risk taking on the turnaround. I could tell he was a bit nervous about my appointment: he had no other women in his management team. In fact, he had no women who were senior engineers – so, this was a risk for him. He never said as much, but it was evident that I did not by default get his trust. I was monitored with more scrutiny, I was asked about how much focus and time I could devote to my job considering I was the mother of three children, and also whether my husband helped around the house and with the kids. I also came under a cloud of suspicion because I had not directly worked in the technical domain – although I had a reasonable working knowledge. However, all this scrutiny was normal for me. The job was challenging and I took it on.

My appointment had an interesting effect on the team. Some of the women approached me and specifically asked to work on technical assignments for me. They felt their technical skills were under utilized in the team. Not using the technical bandwidth in the team did not make much sense to me – especially given the team was struggling. Interestingly enough, I had several men approach me and say the same thing. In fact, I had more than enough interest from the engineers across the organization. I convinced my manager to allow some of these engineers to work for me. I assigned people to projects and project leads based on their skills and interest. My philosophy was to simply leverage the interests and skills of the team to deliver business value.

Diversity came into the picture only in that I did not exclude anyone from participating and I encouraged all those who were capable to take on leadership roles. That is, having diversity as a factor allowed me to take a more inclusive approach in making my decisions.

This was not the case previously. It seemed that the women had mostly been relegated to less critical projects, their technical inputs were not listened to, and they were certainly not put in any leadership roles. The other managers in the group (who were male) were concerned that the women engineers would be distracted with "home responsibilities". Even my manager, who had been forward-thinking enough to hire me, questioned me about my decision to appoint women in lead engineering roles. He also voiced the concern that he perceived the women to be less reliable due to other commitments in their lives. I was sure he thought the same about me. I had to defend my decisions. I said I was not making any choices for the engineers. It was up to them to decide whether they were interested in certain positions. If they had the skills and interest, I will find a good fit. I also pointed out that men were as likely to take time off for personal issues as women. It should not be up to the company to decide which person had the better reason for time off. At the end of the day, any time off is time away and impacts productivity. I also made it clear that I was counting productivity not just by the number of hours someone worked in the office – but, by how much impact they had on the business.

Because I made a commitment to provide opportunities in an inclusive manner, that happened to include more women, the engineers in turn worked hard and produced fabulous results. As a result, my management noticed that they had a very strong set of women engineers and leaders in the group – and it was right in front of them all along. The other interesting thing that happened is that I had more men and women approach me about wanting to join my group.

It was a very satisfying experience to impact the lives of so many engineers in a positive way. I felt I had made a difference.

This is an example of how management diversity in turn fosters diversity in engineering appointments and thereby enables us to maximize the potential in the organization. The starter seed to spark the change requires leadership that is willing to take risk and provide ongoing encouragement.

It takes courage to appoint different types of individuals into leadership positions and to key projects – and not just go back to the default comfort zone of hiring in your own image. The payback is a more energized team that is fully utilized. This results in greater creativity, loyalty, and profitability for the organization.

Ethnic Diversity

The next area to consider is ethnic diversity. The benefits are very similar to gender diversity. In general, software engineering has a healthy share of ethnic minorities represented in teams and in leadership positions. This is a great tribute to the meritocracy in engineering.

However, such diversity seems much more common in some areas than in others – so, there is still ample room for improvement. The following example is a case in point.

> I spoke with Henry, who had recently moved to Silicon Valley. He was an experienced engineer, of Asian origin. I asked him what prompted the move and how he liked it here. He said "I found a job in the Midwest soon after graduate school. My wife and I really enjoyed our life there. Work started out great but I felt I had few opportunities open to me. My job was interesting and I progressed quickly in the first couple of years. After that, I felt I had hit a glass ceiling. There seemed to be no Asians higher than a senior engineer in my area. So, I had to make some decisions and that eventually led to the move. I love it here in my new company and living in Silicon Valley. Besides the weather, the diversity in this area is phenomenal. Let me tell you more about what happened".

Example: Henry's Move

Henry was a seasoned and respected senior software engineer at a large company in their mid-west office. He was highly regarded and a specialist in his field. He had many career discussions with his management about his prospects for growth. They were very supportive and put a career plan for him.

One of the things Henry felt would help was to have a mentor. He especially wanted a mentor who was also Asian and had achieved an executive status in the company. His management set out a search. As it turned out, there were none available in their mid-west office. There were some Asian executives in the Silicon Valley office of the same company. Henry was introduced to these executives by his immediate management.

Through the course of a year, Henry made a couple of trips to the West. The company headquarters were very different from the mid-West office. It was like going into the United Nations – there were people from all over the world. It was eye opening. Henry saw that there was a reasonable share of executives from minority groups. He was encouraged to see that it was possible for someone like him to get ahead in the company. It seemed to him there were two companies under the same umbrella – the culture was very different here.

Henry made a decision to move to Silicon Valley because he liked the diversity in the management chain and had mentors who could sponsor his growth. While he had the necessary support back in the mid-west, it would have been up to him to break all the barriers. He much preferred having a path cleared for him – it made it so much easier.

Henry was promoted to an engineering management position within 6 months of his relocation. He believes that the culture in the Silicon Valley office is what made that opportunity possible.

When leaders hire or promote, the tendency is to hire or promote in their own image. This is not to say that they do not value diversity. They probably do – but, only *theoretically*. When it comes to practice, and when the rubber hits the road – their behavior is to default to their comfort zone: "let's hire Joe; he is more technical than Mary", "I think Frank fits in better into our group". Henry made the move because he knew that he would have more opportunities in an environment that had diverse leadership. People that looked like him were already in leadership positions – that was encouraging. Having a diverse set of leaders makes it more likely that a diverse staff will be hired. This is critical to progressing diversity initiatives – where the goal is to create diverse groups, with individuals that bring different skills and perspectives to the table.

Ethnic Diversity – A Mixed Blessing

Ethnic diversity is however a mixed blessing – for women. Unfortunately, there are many ethnic groups where women have traditionally had a lower status than men. That is, within certain cultures, it is common for women to play second fiddle to the man and even though they may be well educated, be satisfied to stay at home and tend house. When men from these groups take leadership positions, they quite often come with that same thinking into their management role. This in turn makes it even harder for women engineers to get ahead.

Here is such an example. This story was told by Gita, when asked to describe some of the challenges she faced as an Indian-American woman engineer, working in a mid-size Silicon Valley company. She said "I love technology and absolutely love the thrill of software. I always prided myself on my technical abilities. I was at the top of my graduating class. But, school is fairer to women than the workplace. Within a few years of being in the workforce, I found I was falling behind my male peers. It finally dawned on me that I was different from them – I was a small Indian woman. So, I often found myself in difficult situations where the tendency was to box me into the "helper" role rather than the leader role. I am troubled to say this, but this happened more often when my manager was an Indian male. I will give you a particularly painful example that happened to me last year".

Example: Gita's Battle

Gita was a woman originally from India who had completed her Masters in computer science and had been working for three years as a software engineer. She was well respected by her team and hoped to be promoted within the next year. Then, things changed suddenly.

Ram was appointed as the new manager for the group. Ram was also originally from India, and had come to study for his Master's degree in the US. He was considered to be smart, capable and ambitious. However, Gita found that Ram did not encourage her technical growth, and instead kept putting her on grunge work: cleanup projects that were not challenging, taking on more of the bug backlog than others in the team and asking her to mentor more than her fair share of junior engineers.

Gita also noticed that Ram was more comfortable hanging around the guys and had given many of them the plum assignments. When Ram found Gita working late one day, he said to her "Oh, I thought you left at 4:00 every day". In fact, Gita had no commitments whatsoever and focused all her energy on her work. But, the fact that Ram presumed that left her feeling that he thought she did not work as hard as the guys. Another time, she asked Ram about her promotion – to which he replied "You will need to take on more challenging assignments. But, are you ready to make that level of commitment to your work?" Gita was shocked, because she felt she had been doing great work – and had written feedback from her previous management which stated just that.

Gita felt that Ram was very biased against her because she was a woman; he did not understand that women can be just as committed to work as men. Gita became so frustrated she began looking for other opportunities. She found one very quickly and went in to hand her resignation. Ram's reaction was "Are you going to stay at home now?" Ram had once again presumed that Gita did not need to work and did not take her career seriously.

Gita eventually moved on and ended up working for another man – but, someone with more modern values. She had learnt her lesson. As a woman, she already had to fight many stereotypes. Anyone that is promoted into a management or leadership role should be comfortable hiring, nurturing and working with people from diverse backgrounds. As in Gita's case, it is harder for women to forge ahead when their manager does not share modern values.

The impact of all this is that it is critical to appoint people into leadership positions who don't just represent a diverse profile themselves, but are also able to actively support diversity and respect people from different backgrounds.

Skills Diversity – Don't need Ten Pitchers

The most critical aspect of diversity is not how we look but how we think. Being able to bring in different perspectives and value those different points of view is critical for good engineering: it is the key ingredient for creativity and innovation. Yet, it is still common to find organizations where people have been in the same role for five plus years, doing the same thing and working with others who have also been there just as long. It is even worse if the leader or manager has been with the group for that long. These are the same people who might reject hires into the group that don't have a specific technical background or, if they accept the hire, treat them marginally. This resistance to change is an impediment to organizational diversity, creativity and growth. A diverse organization is one that can welcome engineers and leaders with different experiences, background and perspectives – and challenges itself to grow by adopting the best practices from all its members.

I have personally worked with engineering managers that have been in the same group for fifteen years, and engineers who have been doing the same things for a decade or more. They are good people, but they generally don't take risks or drive innovation, or adjust easily to new ideas and ways of doing things. Their leadership does not really foster any diversity of thought – not through any maliciousness, but through sheer lack of experience and inability to lead by example. An organization can stagnate if the leader is unable to stretch the team to think innovatively, take risks and embrace change. Infusing skills diversity into the leadership team is absolutely critical for engineering innovation.

A more common type of skills diversity challenge for a team is ensuring that there is respect for different engineering skills and that the team can cooperate to get the job done. Not everyone on a baseball team can be a pitcher. Similarly, a software team of 10 people can't have 6 technical leaders all with the same specialty. A fine balance of engineers with varying of skill levels and diverse specialties is needed to form a strong team.

> The following story is based on a discussion with Jason, who was asked to share an experience where the skills diversity in a team played a role in business success. He said "I was lucky enough to work for a great manager like Tom – who taught me the value of respecting different views and skills. I was a junior engineer at the time and working in a team with some very talented engineering leaders. Each of them wanted to be a hotshot. Our manager, Tom, wanted to have a diverse skill set since many different skills were needed to build the product. He was clever in how he shaped the behavior of the team leads so that all members were respected and valued. I especially treasured this experience in Tom's team, because I had just left a team where there was a lack of skills diversity, and this basically caused the team to fail. This is a lesson I carry on when building my own teams".

Example: Valuing Diverse Skills

Jason was a junior engineer working in a team comprising of three very senior technical leaders and five other junior engineers. The technical leaders had different specialties: One was a UI designer, another was an infrastructure specialist and the third leader was a transfer into the team from a customer organization.

Tom, their manager, knew that each of these skills was important and had selected the tech leads based on their complementary skills. Almost all projects in the team required these three specialties and the idea was that one of the three would be selected as the lead engineer for each project. However, each felt their skill was more superior and more relevant to the job at hand – and this led to quite a bit of friction among the three.

Tom had to establish a level of mutual respect among them. This was especially critical since he wanted to groom the junior engineers to specialize in each of these areas. It simply would not do to have one area appear to dominate another – since all of these skills were needed to get the job done. Tom achieved this balance by having cross pollination. He had each of the lead engineers gain a hands-on understanding of the other areas by taking on small projects. This helped the leads gain greater insight into the challenges in each area, and as a result they were able to gain greater respect for each other. This also meant that Tom could coerce each of his junior staff to apprentice in one of these three areas, without any of them feeling like they were doing something less cool or important.

The ratio of senior and junior engineers was also ideal: the leads had followers. The junior engineers were eager to prove themselves, and worked very hard to work their way up to the status enjoyed by the senior engineers. In addition, they brought fresh ideas, and challenged the status quo of the seniors – thereby, questioning some of the fundamental design assumptions and evolving the technology in a superior direction. The senior engineers were also able to demonstrate at a practical level what "good work" really looked like, as well as show them the nooks and crannies of each of their specialties. The example set by the leads motivated the juniors to work to that level. This mutual respect, leading by example and energy level in the team, helped form a great relationship among the members and the team was very successful in its deliverables.

Tom was a great manager, who valued skills diversity, shaped the right behaviors, and grew an amazing team.

Before joining Tom's group, Jason had worked in another team that had failed due to lack of diverse skills. There *were simply too many captains and not enough material for all of the leads to prime. It seemed that Jason's manager wanted to keep some leads on hand, just in case something big showed up.*

As a result, many of the senior engineers in the group were leading less challenging technical work. The sharpest engineers left the group and the remaining ones were the "coasters": those that enjoyed the title, but did not really live up to the spirit of the leader role. The manager saw this, but did not take action. He simply did not have the right projects for senior engineers, but wanted some on his staff – just in case.

The inadvertent consequence of this was that any junior staff that joined this team had a low bar to look up to. The junior staff in turn did not contribute very much and were not highly challenged. Soon, the sharp junior staff – including Jason - left. The net result was that the team deteriorated into a pool of mediocrity. The product technology stagnated, the quality suffered and the executives had to enact a turn-around plan.

These examples illustrate the importance of having a diverse set of skills in the team. Setting up the right senior staff, with a set of complementary skills and mutual respect for each other will strengthen the team foundation.

Diversity of skills is vital to problem solving, innovation and just getting things done.

Infusing Diversity into Your Teams

If you find homogenous clumps of people in your organization, you may want to consider shaking things up to bring in greater diversity. Some things to look for:

- Does the head of the group actively encourage diversity of thought and are they comfortable being challenged with different viewpoints from their group?

- Does the group have sufficient gender and ethnic diversity in its management and engineering leadership?
- Are the leaders upholding the principles of diversity within their groups and in their interactions with others?
- Are women from ethnic minority groups being given similar sponsorships and opportunities as men?

As for me, I am an engineering manager with several managers and leaders reporting in to me. I wanted to have a team of diverse thinkers so that as a leadership team, we are able to accomplish more. I set out an inclusive approach to hiring and looked for the best leaders – and not concern myself about restricting my hiring to specific genders or ethnicities. I was much more concerned with having different backgrounds and problem solving abilities in the group. As it happens, I have a very strong leadership team, and one that is very diverse in its thought and problem solving approach. My leadership team does indeed have enough diversity in gender and ethnicity – but, the main ingredient is diversity of *thought*. It just so happened that the channel to getting that diversity of thought was through different gender, cultural and skills backgrounds. Here is my team make up:

- a white male manager, with in-depth knowledge of a core technology
- a white female manager, with startup experience in software development
- a Chinese female manager, with an embedded development background
- an Indian male manager, with a IT support background
- a white male software architect, with industry knowledge of a core technology
- a Chinese female program manager, with firmware development background

Does the diversity make a difference? Absolutely! As a result of a diverse leadership team, we are able to attract a diverse set of engineers to work in our group. Many people want to join our team because they see that differences are valued and respected. The obvious meritocracy is hugely appealing to engineers, and has helped energize and motivate others to join the team and make a difference.

The following is an example of how the diversity within my group has helped strengthen strategy and execution:

Example – Vive la Difference

My team has quarterly strategy meetings where my immediate staff and I spend a day reviewing status of key programs and business goals for the upcoming quarters. In one such meeting, the topic at hand was how we can tackle a new business opportunity. This was a wild card topic presented by Ed, the architect for our group. Ed believed that we absolutely needed to invest in some innovative work to increase impact in our core business area.

A debate ensued over the various benefits, tradeoffs, risks, etc. that would follow if this innovative work were pursued. Ed had walked in with one point of view, but was able to strengthen it through the open debate and discussion. Linda brought up some key technical challenges that would need to be addressed, Mark came up with ideas on how to accelerate prototyping, and Arun highlighted the obstacles such a solution would face in an enterprise environment. The skills diversity in the team enabled us to see a broader range of problems and formulate a better strategy.

The ethnic and gender diversity also played a role. When the topic turned to how we would staff the project, each manager proposed an equally varied set of engineers. There was an equitable representation across gender and ethnic lines in the engineering team for the project. This just happened naturally. The management team did not subconsciously exclude anyone in their decision making. After all, they themselves were part of an exciting, diverse leadership team and saw first-hand the difference it made to strategy and problem solving. In turn, they fostered that same spirit in their choice of team members.

The diverse engineering team made a world of difference in generating creative solutions. As a result we were able to transform the strategy into a viable prototype in record time.

Diversity is a tool for energizing the creative power in your organization – which is vital to high quality, productive engineering teams.

TEAM ESTEEM

How a team sees itself within the company ecosystem defines its self identity and therefore its culture. We are all familiar with self-esteem. It is generally thought that people with high self esteem are more motivated, form healthy relationships with others and are better able to withstand the ups and downs of life. Therefore, they are more likely to succeed in whatever they set out to do. Well, there is a team equivalent "team-esteem". The totality of the esteem within the team, and its self-image, is a huge factor in team dynamics.

Despite software engineering's image as being a fairly egalitarian profession, there is a pecking order. Those on the higher echelons of this pecking order enjoy a higher level of prestige and team-esteem and those at the bottom suffer from lack of esteem. And, guess what? Just like with individuals, those teams with a more positive self-image can attract talented engineers, retain them and in turn produce more innovative, high quality solutions.

Let's look at the concept of team image through an example. This story was inspired by an interview with Lisa, who is a director at a large software company. She shared a story about building a strong team. She said "People need to feel valued in order to do their best. I know that engineers have a pecking order, and those at the lower end of that spectrum, have a really difficult time. But, all roles are important when building a product. If some people are not valued, some parts of the team are likely not as strong as they need to be. One of the things I typically do is make sure that all areas are valued and that we have some mechanisms in place to recognize and reward the contributions in each functional area. I feel that this is a very critical part of building strong teams."

Example: Team Image Problem

Lisa's organization consists of three engineering groups: a development team, a QA team and a support team. The support team was really struggling to deal with customer issues and there were many escalations that could not be handled except with the help of the developers. The QA team lacked domain expertise. For the most part, they were testing to pass and primarily running tests that were recommended by the developers. As a result, the customers ended up finding most of the defects. All in all, the customer facing side of the organization was not faring too well.

The development team on the other hand had a number of superstars, and they were not only meeting all their deliverables, but they also found time to file patents and put new ideas on the roadmap.

Lisa called her engineering managers to see what was going on – why the imbalance in the team performances? She found out that none of the top engineers wanted to be in support. It was considered the bottom most rung, and was avoided by any self-respecting engineer. QA also seemed to suffer from a similar problem. The team was unable to attract or retain talent. As soon as there was any reasonably good engineer, they would transfer into development. When Lisa spoke with the engineers in each of the teams she also found that the drive, motivation and sense of pride were low in QA and support. The team-esteem of these groups was low – and that was impacting the overall customer satisfaction.

A Public Secret

There is a class system within the engineering world that is not much talked about outside. It is the 'Public Secret' – something everyone knows, but does not discuss openly. Just like class systems shape culture throughout the world, so it does in the world of engineering. The type of engineering team, and the perceived technical value of that team to the company, has a huge role to play in shaping the image and engineering culture of that team. Typically, the higher ranking members are associated with the more complex, new areas of engineering and the lower order members are associated with the less complex or the older areas. This is not to imply that they are not all equally important to the company's business, but that is how engineers have naturally partitioned themselves as a society. Engineers flaunt themselves as the most avant-garde, forward thinking social beings. But, when it comes to how they regard each other, there are definitely class barriers.

Image – how you perceive yourself, your team – and how others perceive you – plays a huge role in engineering psychology and culture.

Now, let's go back to our example, and see how Lisa addresses this dilemma.

Example: Lisa Tackles Team Image

Lisa called her managers to a meeting to discuss the business situation. Their product quality and inability to deal with customer issues was starting impact their bottom line. Lisa also pointed out that the support and QA teams were low on morale, retention and this was impacting their effectiveness. The managers all agreed that the class hierarchy in their organization was having a detrimental impact on the business. They discussed how to motivate the engineers across all the teams. The managers came up with a few ideas that they implemented:

- *They created a set of success criteria and career development paths for support and QA engineers, along with clearly identifiable lead roles*
- *They agreed that during rewards discussions, the support engineers would be grouped together as would*

the QA engineers. Their roles were different from that of the development team and ranking them separately ensured that each group had a good share of the rewards

- They also provided some additional responsibilities to the support team leads, such as participating at customer events, gathering requirements for improvements and providing input in roadmap prioritization for engineering. This provided opportunities for strong support engineers to provide leadership to the development team.
- They decided to create a reward system to recognize both the quantity and quality of bugs raised by the QA team and the support team
- They also provided opportunities for all engineers to participate in some level of coding. After all, having some knowledge of the code will benefit support and QA engineers and help them file bugs and debug problems more effectively.
- The managers also decided to hold regular joint engineering meetings with development, QA and support so that all perspectives are heard on ongoing projects and roadmap planning.
- Lastly, Lisa asked that the development teams treat the QA and support teams with respect and bring them into their circle and help grow the technical talent all around.

This new strategy was communicated by the managers to their staff, and after 6 months, vast improvements were seen in the morale of the support and QA teams. This in turn translated to better quality software being shipped to customers and better customer support when problems are found.

Team Esteem Vital to Team Energy

Establishing a strong team-esteem is critical to team dynamics, and enables higher productivity, and quality. Managers must take the lead in building team-esteem by providing a clear charter, measurable goals, and demonstrating how the team makes a difference to the bottom line. When teams feel important, and know that their work has business impact, they will naturally strive to reach higher standards of performance. The drive for higher standards, achieving those goals and having these achievements recognized builds the team-esteem.

A team with strong team-esteem is positive, confident and invincible. That is another key ingredient in setting up a strong community of software engineers that Is able to work together to solve a variety of problems and ship high quality products on time.

TEAM RITUALS

Teamwork is the result of having a group of engineers working cooperatively toward common goals. It is much more than what any one person can achieve, and is strongly influenced by the team culture. As we saw in the earlier sections, team culture is shaped by many factors, such as: team setup, team skills, and team image. All these factors impact communications, motivation, drive and ability to solve problems quickly. There is one more factor that pulls this all together – it is the day-to-day team habits and interactions. That is, the *rituals* practiced within the community shape behavior, transform values into actions, and strengthen the bonds between team members.

The day-to-day experiences of working together, engaging in meaningful discussions, and solving problems, builds the cultural fabric of the team.

Some groups however have trouble mastering the basics of everyday engineering team life – and then that leads to lack of teamwork. The day-to-day interactions are like regular exercise your body needs to stay healthy. These same exercises become critical when struck with a sudden illness – a body heals faster when it has generally been taken care of. Similarly, the day-to-day interactions in a team build a "team cultural fabric" that enable it to become strong: not only is a strong team able to withstand the normal challenges, but can also rise to meet exceptional challenges and come out even stronger. Consider the following example which was conveyed to us by Sam, who is a software engineering manager at a mid-sized company

When asked to share some secrets of building strong teams, Sam said "Building a team is like growing a tree. You need to nurture it, and build strong roots. You also need to be on the watch for people problems and address them quickly. I found a good way to build the roots in my team is to have regular group activities. Simple things like having a weekly team lunch, in-person team meetings, and occasionally team outings are a great way to build this bond. It makes a big difference – especially when the team needs to deal with trouble. And, there is almost always trouble in a software team."

Example: Sam's Rituals Build Bonds

Sam is the manager of a team of seven engineers. As a team, they seem to do a reasonable job of meeting their deliverables and quality targets. Sam thought things were going well.

One day, one of his engineers, Patrick, approached him and said he would like to move on. When asked about the reasons, the main reason was lack of teamwork. Sam was surprised to hear this. After all, he thought everyone got along just fine. Patrick said that almost all communications in the group was by email – and this made it hard for him to ask questions or discuss ideas. He felt the others in the team were not approachable and that the senior engineers wanted to be left alone. Patrick would have preferred to have a more casual approach to asking questions or having whiteboard discussions with the more senior engineers in the team. There seemed to also be a perceived hierarchy in the team where junior engineers in the team, like Patrick, were not included in the casual social circles – such as the lunch or coffee outings. Patrick did not feel he could succeed in the group without the peer connections. After all, a lot of the deeper technical problems were actually discussed during these social interludes. This exclusion made him feel at a disadvantage.

Sam was not even aware of this social dilemma in the group. Certainly, if Patrick felt like this, others must too. Patrick did leave the group. But, Sam also learnt that he needed to foster a better team culture. He decided to do a daily "management by walking around". He would casually drop in to see how things were going and make sure people got engaged together in in-person technical discussions – especially, the newer members of the team. He also arranged for a weekly "walk to the cafeteria" lunch. This weekly lunch was open to everyone. That way, the entire team had a regular opportunity to socialize and get to know each other better. After a few months, he noticed that the team members naturally formed more connections between each other. The junior members in the group began to be more vocal about their ideas; the senior members had more willing and enthusiastic helpers on their projects. So, everyone benefited.

The day-to-day interactions within a team are very much like a web. It needs to be fully meshed to be strong. When the team web is strong, amazing teamwork and productivity result. There is a strong sense of community and pride in the group; people volunteer for assignments; and generally, the team seems invincible. This pays off especially when a team hits troubled times – and this happens eventually to all teams.

In Sam's case, the troubled times hit when one fine day they were informed that the dream project they had been working on was being cancelled due to budgetary constraints. The team was devastated. Many of them had joined the team especially for the opportunity to work on this high profile project and gain experience on the new technology. The other projects under Sam were old-tech and kind of boring. Sam knew that many of his engineers were feeling anxious and there was a strong likelihood that some would leave the team due to the change in direction.

He called the team together for a one day strategy session. During that meeting, he brainstormed with them about all the things that were going well, things that could be improved and what opportunities they had given the cancellation of the dream project. At the end of the day, the team had generated a number of ideas. They also agreed that one of the great things about the team is that they are such a great team – they all worked well together; and, that made a huge difference to their work. They also realized that technology will come and go, but as long as they had a manager that they could trust and a strong team, they should be able to withstand the change and come out on top.

Sam would still have to sell these ideas up the executive chain to get their sponsorship. But, he had the tapped into the hearts and spirit of the team. The web he had built over the last several months had really paid off as an insurance policy against this rainy day event.

It took Sam some time to sell the ideas up the chain. Eventually, he was able to get buy-in for one of the projects. It took about 6 months before the new project materialized. During the interim period, Sam made sure the team felt important and leveraged their talents fully. He also made sure that the day-to-day team interactions remained positive. In the end, the team actually became a lot closer. They had battled a tough battle together. Like soldiers fighting in unknown territory, the "battle" of the engineers against their unknown future and fighting to get the next cool project, brought them all even closer together.

Rituals Strengthen Team Spirit

The one-of big battles tests teams. In Sam's case, the team battled and won. It is a story they can be proud of and will tell many times over as part of the team's cultural history.

The team habits of working and playing together day-to-day provides the insurance for the big battles. Strong teams get even stronger during the big battles. And the weak ones will die even during the day-to-day challenges.

Rituals are vital to enabling strong team spirit – which in turn fuels team health and happiness. Engineers spend a lot of time at work. Creating a fun environment, with meaningful rituals makes it all worthwhile. Simply put, a happier team will be more productive and create better results.

YOUR CULTURAL PILLARS

Great teams are happy, productive and naturally build better products. The key to building fun, strong teams is setting up a community, with core cultural pillars. These pillars are:

- Roles and Responsibilities
- Communications
- Geography & distribution
- Diversity
- Team Esteem
- Team rituals

The engineering team is the cultural epicenter of your organization. Set it up with care, and nurture it. Be vigilant across the six pillars described above. It is easy to get lost in the techno-babble and create a highly complex web of relationships and virtual teams that are mired in bureaucracy. While these trends may align with many current mantras to globalize, decentralize, and virtualize - as well as with the engineering need to erect gadgets to channel communications – they do not satisfy the basic human need to connect. Strong connections are built by human, in-person contact. Connections build trust, relationships and mold the very fabric of engineering culture. This is the secret to building a sizzling team – one that is truly invincible and can tackle a variety of problems, innovate and take pride in their work.

Community pillars are critical to achieving organizational success and reduced costs. A focus in this area will undoubtedly increase team productivity and business value.

How does your organization fare across these community pillars?

YOUR COMMUNITY SUCCESS FACTORS

Here is a summary of the success factors for building a strong community that you can use as a checklist in your organization:

Organizational Success Factors	Your Organization
Nurturing Leadership	
Close knit community	
- Roles and Responsibility	
- Clarity and definition	
- Valued	
** - Communications**	
- % team interactions done live vs. virtual	
- Open & respectful discussions	
** - Geography**	
Single site	
- Team collocation	
- Workspace configuration	
Multi site	
- Motivation: Cost vs. strategic	
- Self contained & fully owned charter	
- Clear success criteria	
- Org structure	
** - Diversity**	
- Gender: staff & management	
- Ethnic: staff & management	
- Skills diversity: technologies, yrs in team	
** - Team Esteem**	
- Team's perception of itself	
- How others perceive the team	
** - Team Rituals**	
- Simple, regular, social gatherings	
- Casual, social connections	
- Team bonds	
Software Soul	
People-focused operations	

Section 4

The Software Soul

Enabling a Strong Heartbeat

The difference between what we do and what we are capable of doing would suffice to solve most of the world's problems... Mahatma Gandhi

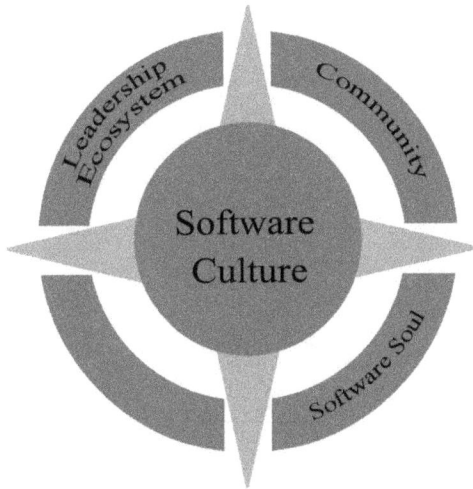

MAGIC ENERGY

We have talked about how the culture is shaped by its leaders, the leadership web and by teams. The culture plays itself out in interactions between managers and the teams in their organization. As a manager, the role one plays in shaping the team culture cannot be understated. Leaders have the ultimate responsibility in harnessing the energy from the organization and enabling a vibrant, "can do", and amazing team. And, an amazing team can create amazing software products and significantly raise the overall business profitability. Tapping into the inner organizational energy makes all the difference between an average team and an amazing one.

How do you energize the team and create that magic which separates the ordinary from the extraordinary? Instilling passion, pride, trust, and creativity into the engineering team will go a long way in fueling it for success. The same organization, with the same people, technologies, deliverables under a cloud of mistrust, lack of ownership, and apathy will not be able to achieve as much as one that is energized. This section will discuss how to create the magic energy that is so vital to transform your team into an amazing, productive and inspiring engineering organization.

The values on which the team operates, the general atmosphere and the rewards and recognition system all play a role in shaping the team culture. Most engineers join a group for its technology, they stay and make a difference when the culture is supportive, and they leave when the culture is bad. There is a significant cost associated with hiring new engineers, training them and making them productive. Although many organizations don't recognize it, there is an even bigger cost in losing a good manager. Managers form and hold the culture – and when they leave, it will most certainly cause a cultural revolution. When an engineer leaves, a part of your engineering machinery just slows down. It takes time for someone else to ramp up, and take over the previous responsibilities. A manager's role is to hire and retain top engineers and unleash their potential. An engineering manager in turn needs sponsorship from their upper management to create a positive and energized culture.

Weaving a supportive culture allows magic to be unleashed – and then just about anything becomes possible.

The next few sections will consider the core values that shape the software soul:

- Internal compass: passion and pride
- Values
- Rewards

The sections will then consider how these work together to unleash the hidden potential in your software teams.

INTERNAL COMPASS

An engineering team fueled by an internal compass is truly magical. The team seems to run on autopilot, with very little required in the way of management intervention. Once the goals and priorities are set, the team charges ahead, battles all obstacles and just gets things done. There is a "can do" attitude, open and engaging technical debates and an unceasing quest for doing the right thing. In effect, a passionate team has an internal engine that creates positive energy and propels the team to achieve great things.

Contrast this with a more regular team – one where the engineers work assignments are managed closely, and where they take their marching orders primarily based on managerial input, metrics and the like. The difference is clear in so many ways. In a passionate team, engineers are engaged, there is a sense of mission and higher purpose; the team has the emotional energy to readily battle obstacles and come out winning. They are charged from within. In a regular team, engineers strive to meet the stated metrics: required bug count, required testing, required code reviews and the like. That is, they do all that is necessary for bean-counting. However, they are not emotionally attached to the mission: they will do what is required of them to deliver the product – without having a sense of ownership and pride.

The emotional attachment to the bigger purpose fuels the passion in teams and that is a critical ingredient for engineering success. How people feel makes a difference to the bottom line.

Passion

A passionate and driven team can easily achieve double or triple the productivity of a regular team. How does one turn an ordinary or a sub-optimal team into a highly passionate and unstoppable force?

Consider the following example, which was conveyed during an interview with Cindy, who is an engineering manager at a large software company. When asked to share a story about the difference between average and great engineering teams, she said "I found that the difference is in how engineers feel. Basically, if they believe in the project, if they believe that they are empowered to make a difference and valued for their contributions – most engineers would go the extra mile to get things done. This is driven by how you feel and not so much by how you think. As a manager, it is really important to tap into the emotions of the team. I have found that this is one of the secrets to a great engineering team."

Example – Energized to Succeed

Cindy was recently appointed manager of an engineering team. The team was developing a part of the software infrastructure, Ngraf, for a brand new product line. The team was meeting all interim delivery milestones, but integrating Ngraf into the rest of the system proved very difficult.

Ngraf was built to the letter of the product requirements, and had passed the required code reviews and testing before entering the integration phase. During integration however, it emerged that the quality and usability of the software was poor and the software failed in anything but the most ordinary of circumstances. The Ngraf engineering team fixed each problem as it was reported, but they themselves did not actively pursue finding the problems. As a result, the partner teams had to drive the integration issues with Ngraf. The Ngraf team seemed to be robotic: they did what was asked of them and barely more than that. Even the fixes to the issues reported were bare bones: they would fix the letter of the problem, but failed to dig deeper to fix the "spirit of the problem". So, each bug fix in turn spawned other bugs and the team seemed to be in a downward spiral.

It turned out that the Ngraf team tested only the very basic user scenarios, and did not think about the entire solution when developing their software. As a result, the problems were addressed piecemeal and the internal architecture deteriorated with all the patch work fixes. This was jeopardizing the overall product development schedule and product quality – and that was one of the reasons the executives decided to hire Cindy.

Cindy was very much aware of the Ngraf team's lackluster performance when she took over. Cindy was charged by her executives to bring things into order and speed up the integration. Cindy was also informed that most of the engineers were indeed technically adept and the team had at one time been highly regarded. So, something had happened and it was Cindy's job to turn it around and fast.

Cindy started by having group meetings to see what the team thought of the project and to discuss ideas on how they could improve things. The meetings turned out to be very disappointing, but revealing. The engineers spent the better part of the meetings fiddling with their laptops: doing email, coding, instant messaging, surfing the web – generally off in their own virtual worlds. In fact, there were a few engineers who just did not show up for the meeting, claiming they were too busy working on their project. They dialed into the meeting from their homes and some from their office cubes. Strangely, the office cubes were typically located within a five minute walk to the meeting room. Cindy was puzzled as to why the team refused to engage. There was an emotional emptiness in the group and a complete lack of urgency and drive. The group meetings were unproductive.

Cindy also met with the engineers individually and tried to get more insight into what was going on. After a few weeks, it emerged that the previous manager, Dan had told the team to "do what they are asked", "don't ask too many questions", and "just get the job done". The engineers had seen a number of issues with the Ngraf requirements and were not convinced that they were building the right infrastructure to meet the business needs. They had voiced their concerns to Dan, but it seemed that Dan had silenced his team. Dan did not want to hear about any problems – he just wanted the team to do what they were told. Dan was very aware that his team had been perceived as troublemakers and "being too inquisitive" and "slowing things down". To calm that perception, Dan had asked his engineers to "just shut up and get to work". Dan's authoritarian style had sapped their creative energy and drive for doing the right thing. Dan owned the project and they were the minions carrying out orders. The project had become just a job and none of them felt that it was heading in a good direction. It also turned out that the engineers had been working in this mode for a year under Dan. So, it was going to be difficult to get them to change their behavior.

Cindy knew she had to change the emotional dynamics in the team and spark some new energy.

Cindy decided to bring in a couple of lead engineers, who were known to be enthusiastic and passionate about their work. An influx of new ideas was needed to shake things up. Cindy also walked through the business framework with the team so they could understand the significance of the project and the role of Ngraf. The team realized just how important Ngraf was to the overall product success. They knew this somewhat before, but no one had ever told them that they were such an important part of the business. This made a difference as to how they felt about their roles.

Cindy ran team meetings with a new set of rules: no laptops, everyone must attend in person, everyone must come in with ideas on how to improve the product. For her part, she promised to listen to all the ideas and she said they will jointly develop a plan to significantly improve the product. Cindy also made it clear to them that she will be evaluating them not just on their ability to do their own work but also on their ability to contribute to the overall product strategy. The team finally understood that their product was critical to the business, and their ideas mattered in shaping its success.

After some initial hesitation, the team actively participated in the team meetings. The two new lead engineers also brought in new life and ideas to the discussion. Within a month, the team had generated some solid ideas for how they can improve the product. The team began to own the product and the results. They did not have to just do what they were asked; they could also have a say in how the product was shaped, how it was designed, and how it was deployed. That is, they could be real engineers again and not just "programmer-bots".

The team had all these pent up ideas, and it was just a matter of tapping into it.

Cindy had made it happen. She had done this by showing them how important they are to the business, why their ideas mattered, why it is important for them to be proactive and empowered them to charge ahead. This made all the difference. The team's morale improved considerably. Their views mattered and they could impact the final product outcome. This sense of ownership energized them to action and they became once again a passionate and driven team. The indifference had vanished and was replaced with a caring and engaged team that was driven to do the right thing.

The product integration began to show dramatic improvement. The team was able to get ahead of the curve and fix problems that had not yet been uncovered in the integration testing. They challenged each other to achieve a higher bar and they did not wait to be told what to do.

The once apathetic team was now engaged in active technical debates, setting a higher bar for themselves and meeting aggressive goals. They had become passionate about doing the right thing, and driving to meet aggressive goals. What a turnaround!

Cindy knew the team was now not only capable of handling this current project but very well suited any set of challenges thrown at them.

Creating a strong, passionate team by setting the framework for *why* something is needed, instilling ownership, and tapping into each engineer's potential is time well spent. Once the energy is unleashed, the team is largely self directing and has an internal compass that will guide it towards success. No amount of external prodding and metrics can bring about the same level of productivity that the magic of passion and drive within a team can realize.

Pride

Another source of energy in the engineering team is pride. Having a sense of pride in one's work and being able to stand behind the product is a sure sign of pride of craftsmanship. A team with pride will strive to excel in its assignments and turn out great products. A team without pride will meet the letter of the operating procedures and eek by on operational reviews, but the product will not shine or achieve its full potential.

So, pride is indeed a secret ingredient. How can one instill pride in a team and make it part of the everyday engineering cultural fabric?

The following is an example of a manager who tapped into the engineering team's pride to create a successful product release.

This story was inspired by an interview with Drew, a software engineering manager in a mid size software company. He was asked to share a story about how he maximizes the team productivity and business impact. Drew said "A key metric I use to gauge the success of a product is whether the team can hold its head up high when the product ships. I ask them a simple question: "Are you proud of what you have built?" Interestingly, many engineers are at first surprised that anyone would even ask this question. After all, it seems a bit unscientific. However, the answers it uncovers are often more revealing than traditional metrics. I have found that tapping into a team's pride is a great way to show them you care about what they think when making big decisions. The team in turn goes the extra mile without being asked. I will give you an example where this was important".

Example - Beyond Milestones & Metrics

There was a situation where Drew's team had slogged for several months on hardening a product for release. They had run a myriad of tests, fixed numerous bugs and passed all the various test and code commit criteria along the way. However, Drew could sense that the team simply was not engaged in the product. It seemed that their energy was zapped and they were simply going through the motions of running mandatory tests and fixing whatever was required just to pass the checkpoints. The team had just successfully completed a checkpoint meeting to assess the final product. The review passed based on the test results presented and the status of the code quality metrics.

Once the meeting ended, Drew asked the team whether they were proud of what they had built and whether they were confident about its quality and reliability. Surprisingly, the team opened up at that point. Most of them said they were indeed not very happy with what they had built. They had taken many shortcuts, and could see glaring holes in the quality. The customers were sure to find out, and the company would be caught up in a series of customer escalations and intense support load.

Drew had suspected as much: his spidey senses indicated that the team was not happy with the product. So, Drew asked them what can be done to mitigate the risk. This started a series of discussions which culminated in a "get well" plan for the product. The release team did not want any further changes to the current product release. Drew decided to pursue the changes for the upcoming release. In 6 weeks, the team was able to execute on the get well plan and had created an image with fixes for the most glaring issues. Drew also alerted his management that it was imperative to get the new image deployed before too many issues were reported. When the first customer issue was reported, Drew's team was able to provide an image with a fix for the reported problem as well as fixes for anticipated problems. This proactive measure mitigated an incoming flow of future issues. Drew and his team were proud of their rescue effort. From that day on, he decided to ask that "pride" question at more regular intervals through the project lifecycle rather than waiting until the end. This proved to be a very effective strategy and one that set the tone for all future projects in the team.

Pride is a source of powerful energy, which when tapped into, can reveal how confident the engineering team is about the product. This, along with traditional metrics should be used to drive the ship/no ship decisions for a product.

The Dynamic Duo

Setting up a strong internal compass within an engineering team and enabling passion and pride in the work will go a long way in conquering a myriad of problems. A team that is guided by an internal compass needs little external prodding, or monitoring. They know what it means to do the right thing and can be relied on to just get the job done well and on time. The reduced bureaucracy naturally leads to greater creativity, innovation and sizzling products.

Pride and passion are a dynamic duo that fuel organizational success.

VALUES

Values are another means to shape the culture within an organization. Most engineering organizations say they value "good engineering" and delivery. There are certain values that are *core* to software engineering:

- Critical thinking and problem solving skills
- Innovation, creativity and risk taking
- Results over perception

These values shape the very heart of the software engineering team. After all, this is what engineering is all about. Engineers think critically about a problem, innovate to solve that problem and build a tangible solution to address it. When these values are practiced, and recognized, teams excel at the fundamentals you have a strong engineering team. Yet, these basic values are sometimes overlooked in the normal rush of building a software product.

Many of the people we interviewed agreed that these are indeed values that their organization holds dear. However, when asked whether these values are actually practiced and whether they are rewarded and recognized, we got another story. In short, there is a lack of congruency between espoused values, what is actually practiced, and rewards: we say we value innovation and risk taking, but don't necessarily reward it – because our perceptions may be otherwise. How can my organization say that they value innovation, accountability and risk taking – yet not reward its engineers for it? There is a gulf between "abstract, paper values" and "practiced values" – and this is a source of tension and sapped energy in many engineering teams.

Ensuring that a particular value is being practiced and rewarded fairly sets the tone for this congruency. If management rewards people that do not demonstrate these values, they send a wrong message about what is really valued, and subsequently risk being viewed as hypocrites. This in turn erodes the trust fabric which is vital to the cultural foundation of the organization.

Let's take a look at each of these "good engineering values" in more detail.

Thinking & Analysis

This is a core engineering skill. Good engineers, with strong critical thinking and problem solving abilities should be treasured. This is not to say they are expert in a particular technology area or a particular programming language. As critical as this ability is to good engineering, we sometimes overlook it when it comes time to rewards and recognition. Many of the managers we interviewed stated that they have been at employee performance ranking sessions, where the management is unable to discriminate between average engineers and truly outstanding engineers.

The following example was related to us through an interview with Sean, a newly promoted engineering manager. He was asked to share any insights he has gained since taking on that role. He said "Promotions and fairness around that process are always a hot topic with engineers. I have personally seen the negative impact on team morale and productivity that comes from promoting the wrong person. I think as a manager you have a responsibility to the team to try to be fair. You have to look beyond just the obvious and dig into what the person has really contributed and the difference he has made. It takes more work – but, that is part of our responsibility. I must say I was impressed by the process in my organization when we recently had to make a decision regarding an engineering promotion."

Example: Peer Respect versus Gloss

Sean was attending his first "people review" as a newly promoted manager. This is the forum where managers can propose promotions, rewards and such. The idea was to table a proposal and have an open discussion among the management team. It was an eye-opening experience for Sean.

The topic at hand was a discussion regarding Dan and Bill and which engineer should be promoted to lead engineer - a prestigious role, with a visible title change.

Bill was a talker. He could solve problems of a given complexity within his area of expertise, but was not likely to venture beyond that.

Dan on the other hand, was quiet, but able to dig deep into the most complex issues and develop effective solutions. Dan had the respect and trust of his peers; whereas Bill was solid, but more of a showman, and did very little in the way of complex problem solving or development.

There was a lot of debate over whether Dan or Bill should receive the promotion. Sean pushed for Dan because he did "real engineering work" and solving complex problems should be front and center in an engineering evaluation. Bill basically packaged the work of those around him, and had not illustrated any strong analytical and problem solving skills.

The managers took a break from the discussion to float ideas by the peer group. Some interesting feedback was received, including "Dan knows what he is talking about, and can be counted on to solve just about any complex problem thrown at him". "Bill talks up a storm. I am sure the managers think he rocks. But, he doesn't understand the fundamentals of our area. This could spell a disaster for our group if he is not kept in check".

This goes to show it may be easy to fool a bunch of managers regarding an engineer's technical ability, but it is very difficult to fool one's peers. So, a true test of an engineer's technical merit is peer feedback and respect. Folding this feedback into performance reviews and promotion discussions ensures the right person is rewarded.

Sean was impressed that the managers had indeed converged on promoting the right candidate. He understood the value of peer feedback. He knew that this sent a signal to the rest of the team as to what was really valued in the organization.

Based on the additional peer feedback collected, the management team promoted Dan. The message to their organization was very clear: if you want to be promoted to lead engineer, you need to be strong technically and be respected by your peers. This is an example where there was congruency between the team value and the rewards.

Example: Complexity Matters

Another example is that not all engineering projects require the same skill level and it is important for managers to discriminate and value the complexity of the engineering task. I was told about an interesting case where the manager was oblivious to this basic fact.

The following story was related during an interview with Lynn, who was a senior engineer in a mid-size company. When asked to talk about what irritates her most about engineering teams, she said "I have been in groups where managers are really not clued into the technical challenges and make random decisions. They have no idea whether the problem at hand is complex or simple and what it takes to get the job done. If you work for a manager like that, then watch out. It will come back to bite you – especially at rewards and recognition time. Here is a story about a time when I was working for a clueless manager."

Phil, the head of an engineering organization, had two very different teams reporting to him: a GUI team and a real time embedded infrastructure team. The timelines for the product were tight and required deliverables from each of these teams in a 6 month timeframe. The GUI team was able to meet its deliverable on time and was highly praised and well rewarded. The embedded team delivered a month later than originally forecast. This happened despite overcoming numerous unforeseen hurdles related to hardware integration, and tackling some very difficult memory footprint problems.

The embedded team was chided and penalized in their rewards for delivering a month late. Phil dismissed the manager shortly after the delivery for not meeting the commitments. This did not seem fair to the engineers. They knew that not all engineering is the same. There are more "moving parts" in an embedded system, a higher level of unpredictability, including race conditions and stringent performance and memory footprint requirements. This level of complexity requires greater analytical skills and ability to solve a more complex puzzle.

The engineers on the ground knew that the embedded engineers were working in a more ambiguous and challenging environment. Yet Phil could not recognize this. By rewarding the GUI team and penalizing the real-time team, the message is that the management is clueless about engineering complexity and is not able to fairly assess the team contributions. This would be like rewarding a runner for winning the five mile race but not rewarding a runner for coming in second place in a 20 mile marathon. This just does not make much sense; but, unfortunately, it does happen.

Management really has to be clued into "technology value and complexity" and ensure its reward system is commensurate with that. When winners of easy races get rewarded and a slightly delayed finish in a harder race is not rewarded, engineers perceive this as being highly unfair. Ultimately, the good engineers will leave the team and the organization will suffer.

Innovation – Engineering Olympics

We spoke with many individuals about how their organizations supported innovation and we got some interesting responses. We found that there were two categories of innovation: innovation that is woven into everyday engineering and innovation where the company has a heavy investment and has showcased the project as being innovative.

Everyday Innovation

The more common type of "everyday innovation" that is woven into most engineering teams is something many organizations simply expect from their engineers. In this case, the engineers were not explicitly given the time to innovate. Instead, they came up with innovative designs and approaches as part of their regular tasks. This type of incremental innovation was generally well supported and rewarded. Engineers who did this consistently were well respected in their peer group and rewarded generously by their organizations.

Example – Raising the Creativity Quotient

An example of this everyday innovation is how one team decided to conduct its development. They created a framework to gather all the team's code every day and do incremental builds, and tests and automatically send results to the team members. This way the team is aware daily of the state of its product quality and can take actions to rectify issues immediately.

An organization that encourages this type of innovation has little to lose and everything to gain. The investment is nothing more than encouragement and setting a higher bar for engineering tasks. The results of this type of investment pay for themselves immediately. The team is energized by the creative process of developing new ideas, and constantly improving how things are done. This strengthens the engineering mindset, raises the creativity quotient in the team and thereby fuels the innovative process. Having this mindset in an engineering team is absolutely vital to unleash the innovative spirit.

Big Bang Innovation – A Mixed Blessing

The other type of innovation is when the company invests explicitly in a project and showcases it as innovative. Typically, an organization sets aside a portion of its funding in breakthrough technology and thereby places a bet on creating the next big source of revenue. Things tend to get a lot trickier in this scenario. The stakes are higher, there is more visibility. This is where the failure rate is most likely, least desirable – yet the investment is also most critical for the company to forge new territory.

The following story was inspired through discussions with several people. They had all experienced the thrill of being part of a brand new, high-stakes, initiative. A common pattern we saw is that there is a tendency to look at the innovation as a means to a "get rich quick scheme".

A typical discussion with an engineering manager went something like this. "I was thrilled to be hired into this next-gen innovative project – at least at first. What I saw was that the executives were simply far too impatient for results and they really had an allergic reaction to any kind of failure. Software engineering innovation takes time – you can't expect results on a weekly basis. Another source was frustration was the marketing team. They had very little to do while we were innovating. So, they became very creative with PowerPoint, and caused a storm of confusion. The marketing team set the wrong expectations, and promised delivery of fantasy features in an unrealistic timeframe. We were doomed for failure from the start."

Example – Innovation Roller-Coaster

An engineering team was created to develop a new, never before-attempted hardware platform with new, state of the art software and sizzling applications that would allow the company to break into new markets.

The team attracted the best and brightest engineers and leaders in the industry and within the company. After all, such a project is a once in a lifetime opportunity for most engineers.

The original forecast for the product was a two year delivery, with an interim alpha release in one year, a beta in 18 months and the final product releasing in two years. As it happened (and as is typical) with such a grand project, which encompassed 100 engineers, it took about a year for the team to have a very basic prototype.

During that time, the marketing team was busy showcasing the product to everyone via PowerPoint charts and generally talking up a storm. When the alpha product finally released at the one year mark, it failed miserably. However, the team learned some valuable lessons.

At this first sign of trouble, the executives became nervous, and started to watch with an anxious eye. Much to their chagrin, the engineering management revised their beta release forecast: they predicted a delay of 2 months and they changed some of the feature content. The team had to change some of the design based on what they learned during the alpha phase and in the process also modify several key features.

The marketing team revised its PowerPoint, but was not happy with these changes. The original set of features seemed much more powerful – and now they were left to sell a less sexy set of features. Such is the reality of innovation: the engineering team had to revise its plans based on what they learned. But, this was difficult for the marketing team and the executives to fully comprehend.

The beta product came out at the 20 month milestone and fared somewhat better than the alpha. The beta rollout had fundamental issues in the integration of some of the applications – which the team had not anticipated. The lessons learned from beta caused another reset to project plans. Some of the core infrastructure components needed to be restructured to facilitate the application integration. This added another four months to the schedule.

The final product came out in two and a half years – 6 months later than originally forecast, and with less features than originally anticipated. There was a big splash at the product launch and customers were waiting. The marketing team finally had its day – although they were disappointed that the end product did not deliver on its original promise and contained features that deviated from the original plans. The customers however were ecstatic about the product and gave it rave reviews.

Despite all this, the key engineering management was fired from the project because the product shipped late and the product was different from what was originally planned. Several lead engineers subsequently resigned since they did not feel that this was fair. They respected their managers and were of the opinion that their team had indeed created a superb product – albeit somewhat different from the one originally planned. But, the execs were not able to appreciate this: the execs saw only that the engineering team slipped its delivery by 6 months and had delivered something that was quite substandard from what was originally promised. They were unable to appreciate the complexity of the project or the fact the team was breaking new territory.

The executives had forgotten that there was a risk element to innovation and this was not a regular project that had predictability. The execs ended up being surprised and agitated rather than being realistic and supportive of the innovation and the innovators. This is what had led the execs to fire the engineering managers. However, this caused the engineering team to lose respect and trust in the executive management and led to an exodus from the team.

As a result, the talent loss sent the product into a tailspin which lasted for another two years. During that time, a new crew of managers and engineers had to learn the product, and support the customers. There was little in the way of new features: revenues were negatively impacted, business suffered.

Failures are Stepping Stones to Success

As illustrated by this story, there are a lot of risks associated with an innovative project. It is the equivalent of "Engineering Olympics" where each of the clever, skilled gymnastic moves is played out for all to see and critique. The difference in the engineering game is that failures are common and a necessary path to success. When this happens, and panic sets in at the executive ranks, the common path is to punish the team rather than rewarding them for arriving at their destination. Punishment could be in the form of disbanding the team, or not following through on promised raises, promotions and bonuses.

Ultimately, this backfires on the organization because top talent is lost from a key product area. At a deeper level, it also sends the signal that innovators are not valued unless they deliver the original vision for the product in the original timeline. This is close to impossible just by virtue of the ambiguous nature of innovation.

Guiding the Innovation Journey

Setting up a reward framework that allows the engineering team to thrive during the innovation journey is critical. Remember, these are often your top notch engineers and leaders. You will need their passion to drive the innovation forward and you will certainly need them to continue evolving the product even after the 'Production Release' milestone is achieved. So, how can you design a reward framework for innovative projects that will demonstrate organizational support without seeming to advocate rewards for failures? You certainly don't want to do this for your established products or lower the bar across the board. However, you must selectively decide which of your riskiest ventures warrants a special reward structure, and set it up appropriately.

Some guidelines are for setting up a successful large scale innovation project:

- Keep the project in stealth mode

  It is important to have time to think, tinker and try things out quietly without sharing the results publicly. This is needed at least until the beta is completed. The more you talk about it, the bigger the expectations. The early days leading up to alpha and then to beta are often the most problematic and difficult to predict. There will be lots of failures at this stage – it is part of the process. So, only commit to the product goals and delivery after the beta is complete. By then, enough would have been learnt from the earlier prototypes and customer trials to reliably forecast what the product content and timeline would be. If things seem really dire, you can also kill the project quietly without too much fuss.

- Retain the Team

  Remember that this is an elite team. So, you need to try to retain them irrespective of the outcome. If the current project does not work out, you will need their skills and the lessons learned on the next innovative idea. If the project does work out, then you will most certainly need the team to stick around and support and evolve the product.

- Restrict the size of the team & collocate

  Keep the team small (less than 25) and collocated so that they can move fast, without too much bureaucracy and communications overhead. If the beta succeeds, and the product proves viable, then expand the team if appropriate. Adding too many cooks early in an ambiguous project is a sure-fire way to slow things down and dampen the creative energy.

- Establish rewards to align with interim milestones

   Structure the rewards to line up with interim milestones of prototype, alpha, beta and the final production releases (rather than just the production release). If the project is cancelled at the beta stage, then the rewards for the production release do not materialize, but you will still have valued and rewarded the innovators. If the production release materializes, but is delayed or has less content than originally anticipated – you can shave off some percentage of the final reward. But, there should be some reward nevertheless.

- Solicit continuous feedback and make improvements

   Engage the team in regular discussion and ask them what they need to succeed. Their success is your success and you will be amazed at their ideas.

This kind of project framework ensures that the elite engineers and leaders that comprise innovative projects are rewarded fairly. When others see this, they realize that innovation for the sake of innovating is highly valued by the organization.

Innovation – Your Future

This is a great example of how innovation in engineering is about setting a goal, being open to change and adjusting the goals. Innovative projects are very ambiguous, and pose high risk since they may not achieve their original goals. So, such a venture is really not for the faint of heart. However, it is imperative for organizations to foster innovation: it is the 401K equivalent of a nest egg for the organization. If you want to have a more secure future, then you better start innovating now.

Investing in innovation is similar to placing a high risk bet in a game. There is no guarantee that you will win. If you do win, you will win big and significantly grow your wealth.

Innovation is a journey that is fraught with failures. It is indeed very typical for a highly successful project to have gone through many iterations of failure before it emerges in the full glory of success. Hence, weaving innovation into the fabric of the engineering culture is difficult indeed. Yet, it is imperative to invest in innovation – else the future is at risk.

Results – Perception versus Reality

Engineers pride themselves on building things: real things that perform useful functions. Building something real is far harder than pontificating about building something. I think we all know this intrinsically, but you would be surprised at how this basic fact is lost to emotion and nonsense in the world of day-to-day software engineering. Once that common sense is lost, decision making becomes flawed, and things happen illogically. This is a sure fire way to sap the energy out of your software engineering organization.

PowerPoint Engineering

Talk and ideology are powerful forces. They are fueled by perception and images, and tend to be far less logical than most engineers are comfortable with. We have seen a number of cases where executives are swayed by perception. PowerPoint is the media of choice for creating "engineering infomercials". There are very few meetings held with executives where charts are not present. This neat packaging of information hides the warts and flaws that are contained in all product proposals. A good executive can still find these through the right questions. But, those without enough experience in the domain, or those under political pressure, will buckle to the ideology and push that forward – balking at any fact that contradicts their view. Software is especially susceptible to this "PowerPoint engineering" because it is widely believed that software is malleable and easier to mold into the thing you want to build. This makes software engineering teams more vulnerable to the effects of PowerPoint engineering and infomercials. The results on the products can be devastating. The results on the teams can be demoralizing to the extent that engineers will leave the team altogether. So, in the context of "tapping into magic energy" – our advice is to use PowerPoint with caution.

The following example illustrates the case of PowerPoint engineering gone awry. The story is from an interview with Walter, who is a manager at a mid size software engineering company. When asked to share a story about how executives can shape the success of a software project, he said "I look to my executives to manage expectations and provide air cover so that I can get the job done. I find many of them get caught up in a simplistic, PowerPoint view of the world. It seems that once a PowerPoint is created, they actually believe that what it depicts is feasible. I think executives need to relearn the art of engaging in deeper engineering decisions and setting realistic expectations. Perhaps having "no PowerPoint meetings" and using the white board will force this. In my last company, a new executive ran the entire engineering team aground by setting the wrong expectations. She wanted to make a splash and used PowerPoint liberally in all her communications. I don't think she really understood the product, or the complexities that needed to be addressed. She just wanted to have a win – at all costs. Needless to say, things didn't quite turn out that way."

Example – Engineering Infomercial

Sheila was hired as an engineering Director a few months ago by Softco. Prior to joining the company, she had spent a couple of years as an engineering Director at a small company, where she managed the development of small scale network management applications. Sheila's current responsibilities included managing some enterprise applications and some real time embedded development. One of the big projects in her team was to enable the embedded software components to be field upgradeable as required by the company's new software standards. This was a whole new ballgame, and one she did not fully understand.

The product marketing team put some charts together to describe the business case, investment required, approximate timelines and potential ROI. It certainly looked like an exciting new opportunity for the company. Sheila was especially impressed with the level of information on the various charts. It seemed that the entire project was well thought out.

Hence, Sheila was surprised when she questioned the engineering team about the project and asked about their confidence level in the plan. The engineering manager, Walter, indicated that the project was risky. There were many unknowns, and he would give the overall confidence level at 50%.

Sheila was stunned. How could that be, even after the entire well thought out details on the PowerPoint charts? She gave Walter a grilling over why the confidence level could not be higher – but he did not budge. Sheila was having a tough time rationalizing the information in the PowerPoint charts with the reality of what Walter was telling her was actually feasible. She knew that Walter had the experience and that she should listen to him. But, she did not like what she was hearing, and she was already sold on the promise of what the charts presented.

In the end, she gave Walter a couple of months to build a prototype and told him to figure out what it will take to make the charts real. Walter and his engineering leads were really annoyed. The charts had been made despite protests from his team on the impossibility of some of the requirements. Walter knew he was competing now with the powerful, wicked spell of the "PowerPoint infomercial".

Sheila was keen to impress her executives. After all, she was hired to bring some order and method to this organization – which had a reputation for chronic lateness, and feature-poor products. She will make it happen – no matter what. Sheila asked the marketing manager to work with her on a road show. Sheila and the marketing manager met with the key stakeholders and executives, and reviewed the PowerPoint charts with them. The executives liked what they saw: it looked like a solid business case with significant revenue potential – if the product could be built as per the forecast plan. The executives knew the projects typically slip – so, they asked Sheila for an even more aggressive timeline and feature set.

As a result, the PowerPoint infomercial was updated to reflect the executives' new requirements and the road show went on. The problem was that Sheila did not tell anyone about the low confidence level from Walter and the engineering team. She played up the revenue potential and ROI, without divulging much of the engineering risk. Sheila was a good talker – so, everyone believed her.

In the meantime, Walter and his team got wind of the hyped marketing campaign and the even more aggressive product plan. The reality they were finding on the ground level did not quite match up with the promise. Walter's team found more challenges, and needed to revise the timelines and resourcing for the project. When Walter shared this at the next checkpoint with Sheila, she fumed and asked that the team put more aggressive goals together. Walter knew this was nonsense and that Sheila had dug herself (and the team) into a hole with the PowerPoint fantasy.

Walter and his team did not want to pursue the project any further as they did not feel set up for success. They were demoralized and their productivity level plummeted. They continued with the project for another few months hoping Sheila and others would come to their senses. When this did not happen, the team members started leaving – with Walter moving on first.

In the end, the project completed one year behind schedule and with a smaller feature set. Coincidentally, this is what was forecast as being feasible by the engineering team. But because it fell far short of the PowerPoint expectations, the project was viewed as a failure. Sheila left the company soon after that.

Fantasy Products not Possible

This story illustrates how even the most seasoned executives can sometimes get swayed by the wicked spell of PowerPoint infomercials. One of the common complaints we hear is that executives are more likely to believe good news and less likely to help when there are challenges. Our guidance is to have an old fashioned discussion at a board with the engineering team to walk through in some level of detail what is and is not possible. Understand the challenges upfront. This will make the engineering team feel like they are listened to, and that their concerns are heard. The point is to continue to have your team energized and focused on solving problems so that you can beat the challenges *together*. Having VP and director level sponsorship makes a tremendous difference to the grass roots. They feel understood and they feel that decisions will be made with the technical considerations being taken into account. This provides a huge amount of energy to the team and enables them to tackle problems head-on.

As for the PowerPoint infomercial, it is an inevitable part of corporate life today. Our advice is to keep it minimal. Just because the pace of software engineering is fast, does not mean fantasy products can be created. In fact, continuing to propagate the myth through PowerPoint infomercials is highly de-motivating and will doom your engineering teams to failure.

Basic Rules of Engineering Infomercials

When dealing with PowerPoint charts illustrating forecasts and product evolution, our advice is to:

- Minimize the fluff and fancy charts
- Create a prototype, and use the white board
- Understand the technical challenges at sufficient detail
- Commit to dates only after a prototype, pilot and feasibility analysis are done
- Create the PowerPoint only after the confidence level of the team is above 80%. Otherwise, it creates a distraction from the real engineering work at hand.

Engineering teams respect and need managers who can make decisions based on facts – and not just on perception. In software engineering, as in other technical disciplines – logic rules!

Infomercials need to be used very sparingly indeed.

Values – Why They Really Matter

The fundamentals of software engineering are all about thinking, innovating and building. How an organization supports these core activities plays a huge role in shaping the engineering culture.

This chapter discussed the following core values:

- Critical thinking and problem solving skills
- Innovation, creativity and risk taking
- Results over perception

When these values are practiced consistently, recognized and rewarded, teams naturally understand that good engineering counts. This in turn weaves these values into the very DNA of the engineering teams. Yet, as we saw in the examples above, these basic values are sometimes overlooked in the normal rush of software engineering and in making easy decisions based on just perception. Taking the time to understand how well your teams are actually practicing these core values, and taking corrective action will go a long way in ensuring a solid foundation for a strong engineering culture.

REWARDS AND RECOGNITION

The last few chapters talked at length about how to get people to work at their maximum potential:

- Find their passion
- Assign clear roles and responsibilities
- Foster pride of craftsmanship
- Create an internal compass
- Practice core software engineering values

Each of these fuels greater energy. When that energy is harnessed, an ordinary group of engineers can be leveraged to do extraordinary things, resulting in: great products, customer service and quality improvements. Once the wheels are in motion, you want to keep it going. A well implemented reward and recognition framework is the engine that keeps the spirit alive. It is a feedback loop to let people know that their achievements are noted and valued. This reinforces more of that good behavior and enables the organization to raise the bar on standards that matter to the group. So, catch your team doing the right stuff and recognize them! This includes individual engineers, managers and entire teams.

Rewards and recognitions clearly show that management is watching and rewarding good work. This is a sure fire way to motivate your organization.

This sounds a lot easier than it really is, and for the simple reason that most engineering managers are concerned with managing "things" and not as concerned with managing people. Engineering managers are trained to monitor the health of their projects through various metrics and take corrective action throughout the course of the project to ensure its success. Contrast with how people are managed in the team. There are few honest discussions, or opportunities to debug team health or people health in the group. We may do this once a year – if that.

If we could monitor the performance health of the engineering team as systematically as we monitor the actual software projects, then we could go much farther in harnessing the full "people power" in the organization. Getting the most out of people means spending time with them, understanding their passions, their strengths, where they need help, and most importantly how they can help the company succeed. A concrete way to make this point is to have a rewards and recognition framework that people believe in and that is simple enough to apply on a regular basis. This is the most powerful way to instill and reinforce the values in an organization.

In general, there are two broad classes of rewards and recognition. One class is the incremental rewards and recognition that happens throughout the year. The second class is the more formal (and more anxiety-inducing) yearly performance and rewards review. Each of these classes has differing impacts on the engineering team. Let's have a closer look at each of these.

The following story was inspired by a discussion with Molly and a couple of her engineers. Molly is an experienced engineering manager, who was highly regarded by her engineers. When asked to discuss her views on rewards and recognition, she said "I believe that you need to recognize good work frequently and that many small rewards are far better than one big reward. We are all a bit insecure, and it really helps to be reassured that you are doing good work. At the same time, it is equally important to let someone know they have screwed up and given them a chance to improve. It is better to do that as soon as the problem happens so they can recover. I found by doing the feedback on an ongoing basis, I am able to get the best out of my team."

Example: Incremental Feedback

Molly ran a top notch team, where everyone strives to do their best every day. When asked what her secret sauce was, she said, "It's all about ongoing performance management."

Molly met with each engineer once a week to build rapport, and discuss project and team updates. About once a month, Molly had a conversation with each of her engineers about how they were doing: what they liked about the job, what was going well, and what they were not happy about. She then gave them feedback on what they could do differently to improve their effectiveness, discussed their interactions with others and got their feedback on how they liked working in the organization. Lastly, she encouraged them to sign up for training or take on new roles as suited their interests or career growth plans.

This monthly dialogue did wonders. The engineers felt their needs were understood, their contributions were recognized, and that Molly took an interest in growing their careers. They also appreciated the honest and constructive feedback on how they could improve: the examples were specific and relevant because everything had happened just the previous month and could be discussed accurately and in detail. This allowed each of them to build on their strengths and rectify any issues soon after it was brought to light. The engineers felt supported in the process because they could also alert Molly to any help they needed from her or the management team. Molly said this made each person feel like they mattered and they made a difference.

The rewards and recognition were a natural follow-on from this process. Engineers were recognized for their work as and when they accomplished something meaningful. Molly tried to catch the people in her team doing the right thing and publicly called out their accomplishments. For example, she would make a point of noting at the staff meeting an exemplary design review, or sending an email to thank an engineer who solved a particularly difficult client problem. She also gave out certificates of achievement on a quarterly basis to the outstanding contributors in areas such as customer focus, quality, teamwork and innovation.

The tangible rewards came when salary increases, bonuses, promotions, etc. were decided: the engineers in Molly's team were not surprised because their monthly discussions had prepared them. They always knew where they stood and how they were doing. Molly's method was great at retaining top talent and driving away poor performers. People knew when they weren't cutting it and left if several of their monthly reviews were not up to par.

Certainly, having regular feedback sessions and ongoing incremental performance coaching is the most effective way to improve the overall team performance. This in turn drives the opportunities to reward and recognize individuals and groups within the organization.

Molly's simple, active management of the engineers in the team and recognizing those that exemplified the team values had a tremendous positive impact: the team energy level was high, the productivity was high and there was a feeling that everything was possible with this team.

In general, we found that engineers were happiest when they were actively managed: good behaviors noticed and recognized, bad behaviors nipped in the bud.

It must be pointed out that most managers do not do this. Molly herself admitted that she is not rewarded and recognized for the ongoing mentoring and coaching she administers. However, it was very evident to her, her team and her peers that there was a "magic ingredient" within Molly's team. The payback was immense to the organization in terms of the gained productivity and morale.

The incremental feedback loop makes a difference. The key elements are:

- Regular performance discussions (monthly)
- Nip bad behaviors
- Recognize accomplishments and good behaviors
- Reward incrementally in proportion to business impact

Drag of Yearly Performance Reviews

Now, let's contrast this with another category of rewards and recognition: a more traditional medium – the yearly performance review. In theory, this is also supposed to be a form of rewards and recognition. It is a time to reflect on the accomplishments of the previous year and reward the individual based on their performance. It is also an opportunity to coach people on areas that can be improved and discuss career growth. But, in reality, it is dreaded by just about all the managers and engineers we spoke with – and at all levels. The reasons cited are:

- It is a lot of paperwork that no one reads anyway
- It feels like you are getting your report card
- It is very political and perceptions count more than reality
- It is far removed from when the actual events took place

Yearly performance reviews are the norm in most companies. However, that does not mean they are effective. Most of the folks we spoke with said they "just put up with it" because HR asked us to get the review done. Neither the employees nor the managers found the reviews an effective way to give or receive coaching, recognition or rewards. In fact, in many cases the review process proved to be stressful, time consuming and, de-motivating. I have personally seen significant productivity drops in engineering teams in the weeks leading up to performance review time and most dramatically in the months immediately following review feedback. Let's look at an example that illustrates this.

This story was conveyed to us by Steve, an experienced software engineering manager in a mid-size company. We asked Steve what motivates his engineering teams. Steve said "The whole rewards and recognition scheme can boomerang on your efforts to motivate the team. I have found that I usually have a dip in productivity after the annual performance reviews. The people that get most discouraged are those that unexpectedly receive lower ratings. Typically, the ones that end up with that are those that are on the cusp between being really good, great and excellent. It is straightforward to pinpoint the average engineer or the non-performing engineer. But, the top 40% of your team needs to be recognized as doing an above average job – which is mathematically true. They are the ones really making a difference. If the definition of average is the middle 70%, that lumps a large number of truly average engineers with exceptional engineers. Putting a bell curve on an exceptional team penalizes good engineers. On the other hand, if a manager has not hired well, then he can label even poor engineers as being in the top rank. Mediocrity rises to the top in this scheme. That is at the root of this problem. I don't have all the answers. But, I am telling you that the current system is penalizing our top performers and it needs to change."

Example: The Annual Review Blues

It was time for the yearly performance review and Steve was busy getting all the reviews done for his team of 10 engineers. Each of his engineers had to spend a few weeks to dig up all the stuff they had accomplished over the last year and write up their achievements in the review. Although in theory this should not have been too much work, in reality took quite a bit of time. It was just not something they enjoyed doing and they also did not see much value in it. They grumbled the entire time.

HR kept sending reminders of the review deadlines. The engineers just sucked it up and did the best they could. Most wrote the review in two hours – after weeks of worrying, procrastinating and just wasting time thinking about it.

In the meantime, Steve's manager had a meeting to do a ranking of all employees. This was done prior to the reviews being completed. At the management level, everyone was already assigned a grade based on each manager's perception of their staff. Steve had a solid team. He recommended that five of his engineers be ranked in the very top, four as average and one below average. When the ranking was consolidated at a higher level, Steve was told he could only have two engineers at the very top and everyone else had to be at level B. Steve knew that putting some of top engineers in the level B category would send a negative message.

Sure enough – when it was time to provide the ranking information and the review feedback with the engineers, the reaction was pretty much as Steve had expected. Only two of his engineers were really happy – those at the very top (level A). Three of his strongest engineers, who were bumped down to level B because of quota restrictions, were very unhappy. They had been told throughout the year that they were doing an excellent job, and they were very much aware of the value they brought to the organization. So, they were deeply disappointed about being rated as average in level B. The rest of the engineers were okay with their rating since they were expecting what they got.

To make matters worse, Steve was mandated to give bonuses only to level A. Yet, three of his strongest engineers were at the top of level B. Steve, like other engineering managers was fully aware of the value of strong engineers and did not believe that a step-function reward system did justice to the contributions of his team.

For the two months following the review feedback, three of his strongest engineers (those rated at level B), were *deeply unhappy. They did not feel like they were being treated fairly. One of them left the company altogether as he did not feel like he was appreciated. One of them moved to another organization and the third engineer took a month long vacation to recover from his emotional set back. The productivity hit on Stan's team was huge. He lost three of his strongest engineers – and all because of a reward system that was flawed.*

We share this story because it is a very common place occurrence. The reward and recognition system has a huge impact on the team morale and productivity. We also see this area as very challenging, and one fraught with numerous problems. Almost any rewards and recognition system is going to have problems. Engineering staff, being highly logical, want something in place that is at least reasonably fair, simple and makes sense. That is, they do need to buy into it. So, the best thing to do is to strive for a middle ground of sorts.

More often than not, yearly reviews result in a morale drain, and productivity hit. There must be a better way….

Rewards and Recognition, a Fine Balance

Rewards and recognition is a tricky area. This needs to be done so that there is some way to reward high performing individuals differently from the average and below average. Yet, when you combine this with the fact that many engineers do indeed consider themselves to be top notch – the results are some unpleasant surprises, leading to lost productivity.

Some general guidelines for a more optimal rewards and recognition framework are:

- Provide feedback and recognition on a regular basis.

  We think monthly is best since it is frequent enough to give feedback on specific items from the recent past.

Focus on some basic questions such as the ones below.

- o How are you doing on your current assignments?
- o What is going well?
- o What are some things you should try to improve?
- o What do you need to be highly successful?
- o What are you goals for the upcoming month?

Keep track of status and progress in a central area for access by both employee and manager. You can also assign a monthly rating to the employee on how they are doing (such as A, B or C). This way, they will have 12 chances during the year to be ranked rather than just one annual review.

The trick is to keep the paperwork lightweight and the conversations meaningful.

- De-emphasize annual reviews

  The annual review is like an exam that you write at the end of the school year. If it counts for 70% of your grade, and you don't do well, then It Is a problem. It is also natural that the month leading up the annual review plays a much bigger role in the rating than the entire year. As human beings, our most recent perceptions about a person play the biggest role.

  Perhaps a fairer way to do this would be to tally the results of the monthly reviews. This would akin to having 12 quizzes during the year. In some ways, this provides broader view of the individual's accomplishments and enables a results-based discussion – rather than just perception in the month preceding the annual review.

  There are no silver bullets. The point here is to spark some thoughts on ways to improve the current system.

- Labels are needed – but painful.

As pointed out by Steve in the earlier example, the trouble arises when someone gets an unexpectedly lower rating. The most common occurrence of this is when a level A person is tagged as level B – due to quota restrictions.

The guidance here is to have ongoing monthly reviews, with incremental rewards, and recognition. The final grading should be part of a spectrum of rewards and recognition.

- Decouple recognition from rewards

    This is an idea worth considering that was brought up a few times. If we can be more generous in recognition and budget our rewards, that might actually address the issues around labeling.

    Josh was in the top 40% of Steve's team. When a numeric evaluation from 1-100 was done, based on his individual contributions, he scored 83. Let's assume that 'A' is for any score between 80 and 100. Josh should rightfully receive an 'A' based on his absolute rating. However, when the relative ranking was done, Josh fell into B – based on quotas. Josh got a double whammy in his yearly feedback – an average B rating and no bonus.

    Instead, if we could give Josh an 'A' based on just his absolute rating that would help with recognition. The budget restrictions could drive monetary decisions. In this case, bonus may only be available to those who had a score of 90 or above. Josh would at least have one positive message for a year of hard work. That is, he is recognized as top talent, and receives his A. Given that most engineers crave recognition as much as (or in some cases, more than) only monetary rewards, this decoupling can indeed make a huge difference in someone's morale.

There may be deeper issues that need to be considered when decoupling recognition and rewards. The example is simply used to illustrate how that can be done and spark discussions on improving this system. The objective is to be more generous with recognition, and budget rewards.

- Provide small rewards and recognitions, regularly

  Small monetary gifts given several times a year, and aligned with specific accomplishments are a powerful way to say "your work is valued".

A Touchy Subject - Leadership Promotions

Promotions and the lack of fairness around how they are done came up again and again as a sore point with almost every engineer and manager we spoke with. This was especially true of leadership promotions – where there is a more restricted quota and a more powerful set of factors to consider. This is not a problem unique to the software engineering world. But, engineers place a high value on logic, merit and fairness. Hence, they expect important organizational and people decisions to take these values as top considerations.

> The following story was conveyed to us by Jake, who is an engineering manager at a large company. When asked to discuss how he handles engineering promotions, he said "It is really important to gather peer feedback before any promotion. It may be easy to fool a manager like me, but it is much harder to fool your peers. I recently went recommended a promoting an engineer to software architect –which carries a lot of weight. This is the process I followed to make sure it was done fairly."

Example: Applause for a Fair Promotion

Jake recently promoted a very competent lead engineer, Rich, to the position of software architect. Jake knew this was a touchy subject. Prior to the promotion, Jake took an inventory of Rich's accomplishments. In addition, Jake also looked at his mentoring abilities, industry contributions, and overall impact to the business. Lastly, Jake solicited input from a team of his current and future peers. The feedback was not all glowing, but it was generally positive and pointed out a few areas for improvement. The question was is the candidate more on par with his current peer group or more on par with the software architects. The fact was that Rich was already working at the same capacity as the software architects – but, without the title and other rewards that go with that. So, based on all this, Jake recommended a promotion. Jake received several unsolicited emails that the promotion was well deserved.

Fair promotions raise the overall bar for performance and expectations in the group. Following Rich's promotion, other engineers started stepping up: they now had a viable career path and were inspired to do more.

Let's contrast with a case where the appointment of a management lead was somewhat shady. This story was told during an interview with Mark, an engineering manager at a large software company. He was asked to discuss how promotions impact team morale; he said "This is near to my heart. I just transferred to a new job because of some shady promotion practices in my previous organization. I thought that doing a good job mattered more than being friends with the right people. Luckily there are still plenty of opportunities in software. If you don't like the way an organization works, you can always leave. My advice for managers is to proceed with caution on promotions and try to be fair. Feedback from the peer group and the teams working closely with the person should be solicited before decisions are made. Let me tell you what happened in my previous job".

Example: A Shady Promotion Pummels Morale

A new program was started to significantly improve the quality and reliability of one of the company's oldest and most profitable products. The executive team, under the VP Jim, was looking for a management lead to drive the initiative. The project would have lots of visibility and if successful, the person leading it would likely be promoted.

Mark had a reputation for being execution oriented. He could be counted on to deliver the most challenging of projects. In addition, he had worked on different components of the products over the last five years and a good understanding of the key quality and reliability issues. Everyone, including Mark, thought he would be the natural choice for this leadership appointment.

Jay had joined the group about 6 months ago. Jay had a shady reputation – but, he was buddies with Jim. Jay was a smooth talker and had a great sense of humor. However, Jay was not a good fit for the job at hand. Everyone knew that Jim and Jay were part of the "old boys' network" and that was a key reason for Jay being hired.

So, when the day came to make a decision for the management lead for this new initiative, Jim chose Jay – not Mark. Jim's appointment sent the message that Jim valued nepotism over merit – and talk over execution. By appointing Jay, the implicit message being sent is "you need to be Jim's friend and a smooth talker" to be promoted. These are not really qualities most engineers aspire to, and hence it shuts them out of the race. Why work hard, when the chances for reward are slim?

Jay's appointment had an avalanche effect on the group. Mark left within a month; his lead engineers left soon after. The engineers that were still in the group spent much of their time gossiping. They were unhappy about losing such a capable leader and strong peers. Jim lost the respect of his peers since they could not back up Jay's appointment. The project got off to a very slow start due to the departure of key engineers. Jay, true to his reputation, was unable to make any solid progress. Jim was forced to replace Jay in another 6 months. Jim was forced out by his peers for making such a poor leadership appointment on a critical project.

Play it Fair

Appointing the best person for the job is absolutely critical to retain the trust and commitment of the engineering organization. These are folks who are naturally analytical and logical. Any appointment done for non-merit based reasons will come under a backlash that will eventually lead to crumbling of the organization and impact productivity.

Creating a fair, merit based organization requires diligence. All leadership appointments and promotions need to be thought out in terms of the impact and message it sends to the group.   Appointments and promotions need to be *perceived* as being fair and justified. Fair appointments can be truly inspirational and motivate others in the team to aspire to the same position. Engineers feel this is possible because the appointment was merit based. On the other hand, appointments that are viewed as unfair tend to demotivate the team, and drive talent away. The message here being "no matter how hard I work and how much I accomplish", I will be overlooked for promotion in this group.

Reward and Recognize what you Value

The rewards and recognition framework is a key underpinning of the value system. It is a critical tool in energizing and motivating your engineering team.   It is also a source of tension in the engineering teams.

While such a dichotomy exists in other professions also, it touches a particularly sensitive nerve in engineering teams. This is because the engineers' world revolves around logical, systematic computer programs that are molded to behave according to the theory of their design. Such is the implicit expectation of engineers about the world around them. There is a belief that the engineering organization will behave in a way that logically, systematically and fairly translates espoused values into practices. That is, engineers expect *fair* rewards and recognitions.

The following is a summary of techniques for rewards and recognition that can help energize:

- Provide regular, monthly performance feedback
    o Tie this into regular rewards and recognition
- Handle promotions with care
    o Peer feedback is a critical part of the evaluation
- Emphasize engineering values in promotions and feedback
    o Results over perception is key
- Exercise fairness in rewards and recognitions
    o Monthly reviews and peer feedback enable this

The rewards and recognition framework is an instrument to shape behavior and garner higher energy from the engineering team. Weaving these techniques into the organizational framework enables a higher level of motivation and team productivity. This is at the very core of the "magic energy" within the engineering team.

THE MAGIC IS THE SOFTWARE SOUL

Unleashing the magic within the software team can result in significant increases in productivity. There are three fundamental factors:

- Internal compass: passion and pride
- Values
    - Critical thinking and problem solving skills
    - Innovation, creativity and risk taking
    - Results over perception
- Rewards

Devising an internal compass that instills passion and pride are an essential first step. This is the foundation for enabling a mindset of "I am trusted to do the right thing and I will do my best to achieve it". The level of ownership and responsibility that the team feels will drive it to excel.

The values must be aligned with the rewards framework. Together they shape the behavior of the team. By valuing and rewarding core engineering principles such as analytical thinking, results over perception and creativity – the organization strengthens its cultural framework. The bar is raised in the team on what is deemed to be good behavior and the momentum is set.

The rewards structure is in fact a mixed blessing. It is often the source of undue stress and lost productivity. A lightweight, incremental recognition and rewards framework will increase morale, and productivity. We strongly encourage you to review your rewards and recognition model and make changes that benefit your teams, their productivity and your bottom line. This is acknowledged to be a challenging area and sadly there are no silver bullets.

In summary, the core of the software soul is all about unleashing magic energy. Creating an internal compass, enabling and rewarding core engineering values and practicing incremental recognition and rewards will significantly boost the spirit of your team.

Here is a summary of the success factors checklist that you can use for creating an energized atmosphere in your organization:

Organizational Success Factors	Your Organization
Nurturing Leadership	
Close knit community	
Software Soul	
Passion: driven to do right thing	
Pride of craftsmanship	
Engineering Values	
- Critical thinking	
- Innovation and Risk taking	
- Results over perception	
Rewards and Recognition	
- Incremental feedback	
- Peer input	
- Manage labels	
- De-emphasize annual reviews	
Fair Promotions	
People-focused operations	

People-Focused Operations

Unleashing the Spirit

We know where most of the creativity, the innovation, the stuff that drives productivity lies – in the minds of those closest to the work... Jack Welch

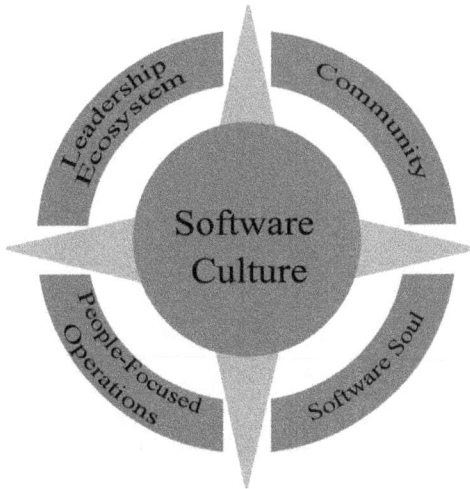

THE TRANSFORMATIONAL JOURNEY

We have talked about the major elements that impact engineering culture: leadership framework, cultural pillars, and the ingredients that fuel magic energy into the software soul. We have seen various examples of failures and the impact failure has on the engineering team's morale and productivity. Some of these are very generic and are not all that unique to software. For the most part, they can be categorized as "people management 101" type items. The point is that these basic people issues are the ones that are most often overlooked and compromised in a fast paced software engineering environment. Refocusing on people, and what makes them tick, will most certainly facilitate productivity improvements in the software engineering team.

One of the main ingredients for success is you – the engineering manager. You have the power to transform your team into a highly spirited, innovative and highly creative group. That is the power of leadership. The transformation starts with being actively engaged, present and truly caring about the welfare of your team. If you have read this far into the book, chances are that you do care! Your personal success as an engineering manager, and the overall success of your business, depends on the success of your software engineering team.

This chapter discusses how to transform your organizational culture and create a people focused operations framework to unleash the full potential of your software teams.

There are three basic steps needed:

1. Baseline the team pulse – the organizational success factors
2. Determine what is working, what is not, and what must change
3. Monitor the team pulse regularly and take corrective action

It is important to understand where you are, what is working, and what you need to do to be successful. This is a *continuous* activity - not a one-shot deal. It is an ongoing effort to monitor the pulse and maintain a healthy organizational heartbeat.

Let's discuss how to create a healthy team pulse.

THE ENGINEERING TRIUMVIRATE

The engineering team effectiveness relies on three fundamental pillars:

- people
- technology
- operations

The engineering manager needs to actively manage across all these dimensions in order to maximize the team impact. The manager gets assistance in operations and technical decisions from advisors and experts. For operations, program managers provide guidance to achieve greater operational effectiveness. For technology, technical leaders and architects provide guidance and advice on technical issues. Ultimately, the engineering manager needs to make the technical, operational, and people decisions. They only have advisory help in two of the three important dimensions. The third pillar – people – is perhaps the most important pillar, but does not have a recognized advisory role within engineering organizations.

People management is largely left as an afterthought. It is expected that the engineering manager will *naturally* do the tasks required for managing their team effectively. Yet, time and again, we see that an underlying theme for software project failures is the inability to fully harness the power of the engineering team. This causes entire organizations to implode, and programs to fail. There are very few engineering managers that *naturally* focus on people management. Many are simply too busy managing projects, and many believe that people management is not really valued by their organizations. By and large, engineering managers do not spend the necessary time on team management. Perhaps the heavy emphasis on technical skills and the scarcity of those skills make us "look the other way" and just get by with weaker people skills in engineering managers. Whatever the case may be, engineering managers are getting help and advice in two critical dimensions of their business: technology and operations. They seldom – if ever – get help on fully leveraging the power of their teams.

As a result, the most important dimension - people- with the most valuable set of assets, is typically the one that receives the least attention.

A new advisory role is proposed - the Team Effectiveness Coach, who will guide the engineering manager on 'people focused operations'. The engineering manager retains the overall ownership for team effectiveness, but can leverage the coach's assistance in influencing change and enabling a more positive culture. The objective of this role is to enable a greater awareness of the team pulse, and increase team effectiveness. This role will improve the decision making in areas such as staffing, morale, teamwork, and leadership, resulting in greater productivity.

Ultimately, this role completes the advisory triumvirate for engineering leadership: operations, technology and people issues will each have a specialist. Each of these specialists develops strategies, and follows through by implementing plans to maximize business success.

The role does not necessarily entail a separate job function. An experienced engineering manager or program manager can also take on this additional responsibility – provided they have the necessary background, aptitude and time. A basic requirement is that the person has a strong track record of growing engineering teams and has experience in resolving the typical conflicts, dramas and challenges of the engineering environment.

The role itself could fold into a central program management organization. Where this is not possible, or where the situation requires a more objective evaluation, it may be desirable to bring in a third party to fulfill the role. Some judgment needs to be applied as to which mechanism best suits the organization. For example, a third party may be required when there are sweeping changes planned, when there have been long-standing team problems, or when teams are merging or being disbanded. These larger organizational changes often require an objective evaluation of how best to maximize the transition. In other cases, if the people issues are contained to a specific team or project, an experienced program manager or senior engineering manager can perform this function. Whoever performs the role, the role itself is unique in that its main objective is to bring focus to the people issues and maximize the team's full potential.

The next section will discuss the role of the Team Effectiveness Coach (TEC) in more detail.

THE TEAM EFFECTIVENESS COACH

As we have seen in numerous stories in this book, business failures result when there is inadequate attention paid to people issues – that is, how people feel about their jobs and their teams. Tuning into the team pulse, analyzing weaknesses and taking action can make it more likely that bad situations can be turned around. The question is how to do this in the fast-paced world of software engineering – where managers have their hands full with shipping products and where they may not have the necessary skills or interest in dealing with such issues.

The role of Team Effectiveness Coach (The TEC) is to focus on people issues. The TEC's primary objective is to enable a vibrant team pulse. The TEC functions in an advisory capacity to the entire engineering team and is the catalyst to create a well balanced, happy and productive team.

Let's explore the role of the TEC in more detail.

The TEC Role – a closer look

The concept of a coach is not new to the business world or to software engineering. There are some well known coach roles already in existence: executive coaches, organizational coaches and agile coaches. These coaches work within certain spheres of the organizational framework. The executive coach counsels executives on their personal growth. The organizational coach provides guidance on organizational structure and process. The agile coach provides guidance on agile development methodology and enables operational practices that improve the velocity of developing software products.

The TEC complements the activities of these other coaches. The TEC counsels the entire engineering team on handling the people issues that permeate the engineering organization. The TEC will address issues such as how to improve teamwork, communications, collaboration and trust. The TEC's focus is on continually improving the team pulse to unleash the spirit of engineering teams.

Unlike an executive coach or an agile coach, the TEC needs a very strong background in software engineering management, with a track record of growing productive teams and a passion for maximizing the engineering spirit. The TEC is a *practitioner* with a strong track record of success. While agile coaches and executive coaches have their place in the organization and provide much added value, the TEC operates at the very nucleus of the engineering team – the people.

The following diagram illustrates the relationship between the TEC and other types of coaches:

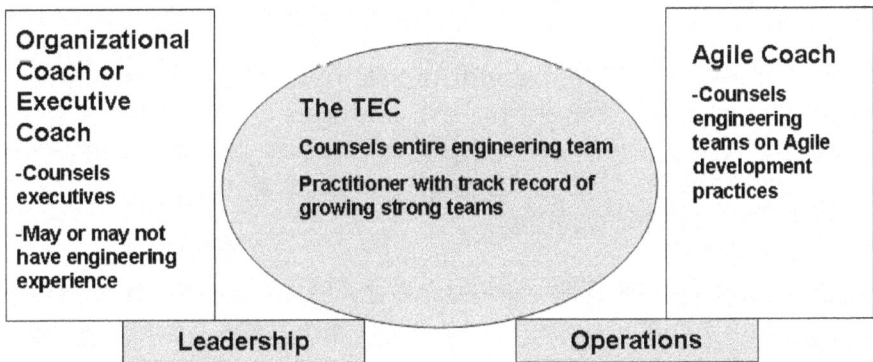

Organizational Coach or Executive Coach

-Counsels executives

-May or may not have engineering experience

The TEC

Counsels entire engineering team

Practitioner with track record of growing strong teams

Agile Coach

-Counsels engineering teams on Agile development practices

Leadership   Operations

The TEC works across the entire engineering organization and accelerates the discovery and resolution of people-related issues.

Typical responsibilities of the TEC include:

- Counseling the engineering team on people issues

- Base lining the team pulse
- Providing regular team diagnostics reports and analysis
- Proposing remediation plans, and driving implementation
- Participating & advising on hiring & organizational changes
- Participating and advising on changes to team operations.

As pointed out earlier, the TEC is not necessarily a separate job function. It is a unique role, with a strong people focus. It can be fulfilled by an experienced engineering manager, a program manager or by a third party. In day-to-day operations, training the engineering and program managers to fulfill this expanded role would be an ideal way to enable this focus.

If the people issues are more controversial or long-standing, it may be appropriate to bring in an impartial third party TEC. When the coach is a third party that comes into the organization, it is best to have that person work closely with the team for an period of time – such as 3 to 6 months - so they understand what really makes the team tick, provide recommendations and participate in guiding and implementing the changes. It can't just be a "one-off" engagement. The TEC needs to gain a deeper understanding of the team dynamics and participate in enabling greater change.

Some have said "HR should be doing this, but quite often they don't really understand how engineers work", or "We only talk to HR when things are really problematic and over the top." Another comment heard is "We need someone who can spend some time with the group to understand what is *really* happening here". Also, HR is sometimes viewed as the last resort. You only involve HR in dire situations or if there are legal issues. As we saw in many examples, waiting until the situation is dire can significantly impact business; and very few of these situations are legal issues – just *ordinary* people issues that get out of hand and hamper progress. The idea is to catch the people issues while they are still simmering.

Team Diagnostics

There needs to be a way to gauge the team effectiveness and team pulse. How healthy is the team, and are they working at their potential? A simple process is needed to monitor this on a regular basis, identify issues and take action. A diagnostic report consolidated on a regular basis by the TEC is suggested to gather this information. The diagnostic report could be a consolidation of the Success Factors Checklist listed at the end of each chapter. These checklists are very detailed.

Alternately, you can have a more compact form of the diagnostic report that provides a window into the team pulse. Here is an example:

Topic	Team Perception	Management Perception	Comments
Leadership ecosystem	3	5	
Community mindset	3	5	
Communications strength between leaders and staff	3	5	
Team feels like they are set up to succeed	4	4	
Cooperation	4	4	
Team Energy	3	3	
Team Esteem	3	3	
Diversity	3	2	
Fairness in rewards and recognition	2	4	
Innovative spirit	3	3	

In the table above, the team perceives a lack of fairness in rewards and recognition (rated 2), whereas the management team perceives it is fine (rated 4). The discussion around what these numbers mean and why there is a gap is the real benefit of this report. It brings people together regularly to talk about factors that shape human behavior in an organization. This activity brings issues into the open and offers an opportunity to improve the team culture.

The purpose of the report is to spark a regular dialogue about people issues and create a forum where the engineering team can discuss what is going well and what needs to be improved. Any troubling issues that crop up can be dealt with promptly before they get out of control and seriously impact the team productivity and morale.

The team diagnostics have a direct influence on organizational and product success. Early in the book, we introduced the software business diagnostics as a means to measure overall product success. Note: refer to the section on "Framework for Software Success" for a sample software business diagnostics report, which describes the outcome of David's software adventure. The TEC can analyze the data from software business diagnostics and the team diagnostics on a regular basis and look for trends, correlations, and opportunities for improvement.

The TEC will hold regular discussions with the engineering team to review these reports and recommend action plans. This process can be thought of as a continuous integration of the engineering team health. Although such a report can be automated through surveys and anonymous reports, it is recommended to have the TEC do the monitoring and reporting through dialogue with the engineering team. Much of our communications is non-verbal, and a human being is more likely to pick up on the nuances of what is working well and what needs improvement versus a strictly automated report. When the stakes are high – as it often is in turning around a poorly performing team – the TEC can partner with line management to significantly accelerate the discovery of people problems and suggest optimal ways to address them.

Establishing a Strong Team Pulse

Let's revisit the three areas that need to be addressed to create and maintain a healthy culture.

1. Listen and Understand

The TEC engages with the entire engineering team to assess the health of the team pulse. Regular diagnostics and discussions with the team help set the base line. This is the launching point for further discussions on how to improve team culture.

2. Which Problems will you fix?

The team coach will report the findings and hold a discussion with the management and engineering team. The point of this exercise is to establish a joint understanding of what is going well and what needs to be improved.

The list of things to improve must be small and actionable in order to have traction. There will always be lots of things to improve. The point is to select those items which are most critical to your team.

For example, if the team energy is low and the attrition rate is high – this item is a much higher priority to address than improving the innovative spirit. Without a team, there is no innovation.

3. Keep the Team Healthy

Monitor the organizational heartbeat and culture regularly and take action to fix issues promptly.

This is the perhaps the most important message. Culture is like air – it is there all the time and is part of everything you do. If you have worked hard to get things in order and are happy with your culture, you should also work hard to maintain it.

The next few sections provide examples of the Team Effectiveness Coach in action. Unlike other examples in this book, these examples are more speculative: what might happen if we had a TEC role in the organization? The purpose of these examples is to illustrate the potential benefit of a TEC to organizational culture. The examples we will consider are:

- Strengthening the Leadership Web
- Catalyst for Diversity
- Guiding Changes in Charter
- Promoting innovation
- Establishing a quality mindset

Lastly, we will revisit "David's software adventure" and discuss how a TEC may have mitigated some of the issues by fostering communications, collaboration and balanced decision-making.

TEC - STRENGTHENS LEADERSHIP WEB

The following example demonstrates how the TEC provides insight into organizational dysfunction by acting as a liaison between the grassroots team and the head of engineering. It also illustrates how the TEC works with the executives to plan and drive leadership changes that will have the team's buy-in. The TEC takes the team from a point of dysfunction to a point of health by observing the team, identifying people issues, recommending actions, and driving their implementation.

George's VP team was under pressure to become more productive and cut costs. The general sentiment outside the group was that it was a large group that moved too slowly, had a bunch of reject engineers and was not adding value to the company. The VP decided to bring a team effectiveness coach as a means of accelerating productivity improvements in the team. The VP's aim was to revitalize the group and make it a productive part of the company once again.

The TEC, Ron, was a respected third party consultant, who had experience with assisting such ailing organizations. Ron had worked as a software engineering manager for many years, and had a track record of building strong teams. His experience had given him insight into what makes engineering teams tick, and how to maximize the team's potential to achieve remarkable results.

Ron started by sending an email and stating his mission to the entire team and invited anyone who was interested to come in and talk with him. Many of the management and engineering staff took the opportunity to speak with Ron. They gave him candid feedback about what was working well and what was not working. They made recommendations about how things could be improved. After about one month, Ron had collected enough information to do a baseline team diagnostic report.

Ron also met with stakeholders such as upper management, key client teams and partner teams to understand their perspectives.

Ron then called a meeting with George to discuss his preliminary findings. Many of the issues pointed to failings within the management team. The one exception was Doug – who everyone thought was doing an outstanding job.

Doug was known to be a very competent engineering manager with strong people management skills. His team had a reputation for top notch delivery, attracting and retaining strong talented engineers, and creating breakthrough innovations. Unfortunately, the rest of the teams were languishing. Obviously Doug was doing something right that the others needed to emulate.

Although Doug was highly respected, it seemed that several of the other managers were not respected by their teams. Some of them had no drive, no pride, and some did not even meet with their teams regularly to understand what their groups were doing. Hence, many of those teams ended up doing whatever they liked and the strong performers in those teams felt like there was a very high tolerance for poor performance – something they found unacceptable. Many of them pointed to Doug as the kind of manager they would like to have. Ron also found that the management team lacked diversity and hence many of the engineers came from the same backgrounds as their immediate manager. Lastly, he found that none of the teams, except Doug's team, were proud of their work. They felt like they were working on things that did not matter, and were not clear of the value they added to the company's bottom line. Certainly, their managers did not make this clear to them. As for the managers, Ron found that many of them lacked the drive and viewed their job as a "retirement post". They were not taking it as seriously as they should. They had brought in engineers who were also on the "retirement path" – and this had brought down the energy level of the entire team.

George formulated some organizational and staffing changes based on Ron's input. Ron provided guidance throughout the process. Ron's impartiality was very valuable to George. Ron was able to make assessments of people, their skills and their potential based on his own experience as well as his discussions with the team. Ron was able to provide a grassroots perspective directly to George. George knew this view would have been very difficult to gather on his own or through his management team. This gave George more confidence in bouncing ideas around with Ron, rather than just talking to his management team – many of whom would have a vested self interest.

George and Ron developed several options. Ron then helped by floating proposals in confidence to some select individuals in the team as well as trusted stakeholders, to solicit their input. He played out some "what if" scenarios with these individuals. This in itself provided an energy boost to the team. They saw that their inputs were making a difference and some changes were being considered. After about two months, the organizational changes were rolled out.

George also requested that Ron provide hands-on coaching to one of his managers to help inject more energy in his leadership style and into his team. Ron agreed that this would make a positive difference and reached out the concerned manager to work out a plan and put it into action.

Ron stayed on board for a few more months with the team. During that time, he took regular checkpoints on the state of the culture, and how things were evolving. It took 6 months for the situation to achieve equilibrium and for the team to become fully productive. Ron was asked to continue the checkpoints for another year and provide *ongoing guidance on how to maintain a healthy culture in the group.*

The TEC, Ron, provided valuable insight to George about the real feelings of the engineering team. George was able to leverage this information, and work with Ron to float some ideas about potential changes. Ron's vast experience in growing strong engineering teams was crucial. He was able to provide George guidance on what changes would work, what types of leaders would be respected, and so on. In addition, Ron stayed with the team to see how the changes took effect and provided mentoring to George and the entire team through the process. This ensured open communications through a critical time in the organization. The inevitable hiccups were ironed out quickly and as a result, the changes rolled out relatively smoothly.

TEC – A CATALYST FOR DIVERSITY

The TEC can act as a change agent in the interests of the company to uphold values and drive change into the operational framework. For example, if the company is actively trying to promote diversity, but is finding it challenging because "there are simply not enough qualified women" – then, they may want to request the help of a TEC to raise awareness and spark the necessary changes. It might just take an objective third party to sponsor the hiring someone 'not in the image' of the rest of the management team, but someone that can bring fresh ideas and thoughts to the organization.

An example that was encountered during the interviews is that of a new head of engineering who had an opportunity to fill several engineering management positions. He filled four out of the five positions with Indian males and one with a white male. The white male in turn hired four white senior engineers. The Indian males hired other Indian male engineers. In the midst of all this, the one woman engineering manager left and took a role in another organization.

When such obvious "diversity inertia" happens in an organization, or when women feel that they need to leave because the old boy's network is getting even tighter, someone needs to raise a red flag. In all likelihood, these hires were not bad. But, the hiring process was definitely not *inclusive* in that it did not consider all possible candidates, and the opportunity was not used to exercise diversity.

Hence, some spark is needed to break this cycle of default behavior.

Now, let's look at how diversity can be *actualized* into the operational framework. The team effectiveness coach acts as a catalyst for this change.

TEC Sparks Diversity in Leadership

The head of engineering is considering making some leadership changes in the next 6 months and solicits the input of the TEC. The TEC does a baseline evaluation of the organization – including diversity. The coach presents this data to raise awareness of the current team composition.

The TEC points out that in the current organization of 20 engineering managers, there are two female engineering managers. The rest are all male, with 70% of them being Asian male. The coach also points out that the engineering staff has about 25% females and there is under-representation of females at the management level. The TEC had also been gathering regular organizational diagnostics. These reports clearly showed that the team perceives that there was not sufficient diversity.

The TEC has created a spark. There is data brought forward on the current makeup of the organizational leadership. The conversation creates awareness of the current situation and opens a dialogue about what some of the possibilities are. That is the first step.

During the next quarter, as the organizational decisions are being made and people are being interviewed for the various leadership positions, the TEC plays a monitoring and guiding role. For example, if three candidates interview for a management position and all have different strengths and weaknesses, and the recommendation is to hire an Asian male, the TEC will ask pertinent questions regarding whether someone else might be more appropriate. If, as is usually the case, where the people making the decision "choose in their own image", the TEC will be a catalyst for upholding diversity and challenge the decision. The TEC's experience as a practitioner gives him the credibility to challenge such decisions – since he has the background to assess engineering leaders. The final decision still rests in the hands of the hiring manager, but the TEC will ensure that decisions that impact the company's cultural values are made with full awareness. As we know, without that spark and catalyst for change, the default behavior is to keep things inside the comfort zone.

It is the expectation that such awareness-raising by the TEC during the hiring process for leadership positions will cause at least some subset of the positions to be filled by a candidate that may not have been the obvious default choice – but, someone that needed additional sponsorship in line with the company's diversity values. In turn, this will bring a fresh perspective and compliment the experience of the existing team.

The TEC's role here is to ensure the organizational values are translated into action in the operational framework. Many companies have people-oriented initiatives that take years to roll out. A TEC can help accelerate changes by providing guidance and feedback throughout the process.

TEC – GUIDES CHANGES IN CHARTER

There is often a lot of drama when changing the charter of an engineering team. Quite often, engineers who have been with the old program for a while are reluctant to either give up their charter or take on new roles. In this kind of change, it is easy to lose the team spirit and impact productivity. A TEC can guide such changes with minimal impact.

The next story illustrates the role of the TEC in transforming a team of crusty old timers into a motivated team for a new program. It shows how the TEC partners with the management team to hire the right leader and guide the team through the transition without impacting morale – and keeping the business on track.

TEC Infuses Diverse Skills in the Team

Chuck had just taken over as manager for a team of 10 engineers. The team had remained largely intact for the last five years and had a solid reputation for delivering good products. Chuck had accepted the job as manager because the executives wanted to transfer the current product - Cprod- to another team and take on a new program - NPro. Npro would radically change their core business and bring in a much needed source of new revenue. The problem was that the engineering team seemed reluctant to move on. They were very attached to what they had been doing.

The TEC, Ron, had been with the organization for a couple of months and observing the team. Ron was impressed by their engineering prowess. They were bright, hard-

working and generally happy. However, he found them to be very insular and not very open to new ideas. In fact, the team rarely interacted with those outside their immediate group. They were content to continue working on Cprod and were reluctant to transfer the product to another group. In fact, Cprod had been polished to the highest degree and Ron's sense was that the team was inventing things to improve on an already great product – rather than looking for new opportunities and going where the business need is.

The executives wanted to embark on the new program, NPro, with this strong team of engineers. They knew that the charter change would be very sensitive. The executives did not want to lose the engineering team, and that was why they requested Ron's help during the transition. Ron had informed the management about the engineering team's passion for their old area and that it was going to be challenging to bring about change. Hiring the right manager would be critical.

Ron participated in the hiring process and was influential in hiring Chuck. Chuck had just the right personality. He was a good listener, open to debates, patient and technically strong. Most importantly, he had a track record of managing senior engineering teams. During the interview, Ron played out some "what if" scenarios of how Chuck might introduce change into this team. Chuck indicated he would start by valuing the team's accomplishments, understand their interests, and build trust. This will take a few months. Change can only come after that. Ron liked what he heard. Still, it would be a tough road ahead for Chuck: these were crusty engineers.

Ron worked with the team to understand their interests, their fears, and play out some "what if" scenarios. By the time Chuck started in the group, Ron had a game plan for him. Ron advised Chuck to refocus only five of the engineers on NPro. They were more open to learning new skills and were looking for growth opportunities. Ron suggested that the other five engineers remain on the old product for a bit longer. These engineers had been with *the Cprod the longest. They were also worried about losing their seniority and having to start all over again on something brand new. They were not so sure about making the change. Ron understood this, and continued to discuss these fears with them. Ron also kept the executives in the loop regarding the team dynamics and the need to phase in a few engineers at a time to NPro – rather than an immediate switch. Ron advised this was necessary to keep a balance between business needs and team needs.*

Chuck followed Ron's advice and ramped up the five engineers. Over the course of the next couple of months, Ron was able to convince two more engineers to transition to NPro. Ron advised that the remaining three engineers transfer to the new team with Cprod. They were simply too attached to the old product and were not at all open to learning new skills. Ron felt that forcing them to move would severely impact their morale as well as the rest of the team's. The management followed Ron's advice. In time, they found more engineers willing to join NPro.

Ron's advice played a critical role in the team transformation. Ron's experience and insight into the engineering people dynamics of the team were critical in guiding team decisions and setting the business on the right track.

The role of the TEC is critical in transitioning the engineering team smoothly from their existing roles to new roles. An engineering team needs to be mentally prepared to diversify its skills to meet changing business needs. However, engineers often expect the worst in times of change, and keeping them engaged in the change process, soliciting their input is very much necessary to keep the team spirit intact. There is uncertainty, fear and stress involved in any type of change. Many of the interviewees we spoke with indicated that attrition is highest in times of change.

A TEC can work with the engineering team through role changes to ensure a smooth transition – and keep the team and the spirit intact.

TEC – ESTABLISHES QUALITY MINDSET

We are all aware of how important quality Is to a software product. There are numerous metrics and methodologies that have been put in place to help achieve good quality. This is very much necessary. However, there is a sense that measuring all the metrics and methodology alleviates the need for true responsibility. Responsibility for quality *goes beyond the metrics*. Just because the numbers look good, doesn't necessarily mean the product is good. Most engineers are aware of this basic fact. Each person, each engineer, each manager on the software team needs to be *committed* to really delivering a quality product. To get to the heart of the matter, there needs to be a broader evaluation of the product – beyond metrics – to fully evaluate the product quality.

The TEC, who takes on the role of people-focused operations, can help the team go beyond these metrics. The TEC can bring about changes to the decision making process surrounding the product development cycle. The TEC will do this by tapping into the hearts, behaviors, and human elements that shape product quality. The simple idea is that the engineering team's *stories* and *perception* about the product state, its quality and its readiness are just as important to making business decisions as raw metrics.

One such area where the TEC can play a role is actually *instilling a quality mindset into the product lifecycle.* This is described in the next section.

Quality Mindset in the Product Lifecycle

There are specific *behaviors* that can promote a *quality mindset* within the organization. These behaviors come into play at each step of the software product lifecycle. A TEC is the catalyst for behavior change and can help weave the quality culture into the very fabric of the group.

Let's take a look at the standard product lifecycle and see how the TEC can help spark the right quality mindset by asking a set of leading questions, prompting discussions, and providing guidance. The coach's job is to guide the human elements and behaviors that shape product quality. The TEC will solicit free form input from the engineering team throughout the product lifecycle – as part of gathering the regular diagnostics.

These leading questions would be asked directly or inferred through discussions with the engineering team.

Logistically, the TEC will gather information about the *team's* perception of the product quality. This will complement the standard project related metrics. This data will be tracked and communicated to the decision makers so that they can make more informed business decisions.

The TEC may ask the engineering team open ended questions such as those listed below:

- Is everyone aligned on the mission ahead?
- Does the engineering team believe it is set up for success?
- Is everyone fully engaged in building a good product?
- Is there cooperation between the team members?
- Is everyone on the team doing what it takes to ensure a high quality product?
- Are there constructive, open debates?
- Is management open to feedback – especially bad news?

- Is the team able to rally quickly to solve problems?
- What can be done to help the team work more effectively on delivering a quality product?
- What is your confidence level in the product quality?
- Are you proud of the product you have built?

Heartfelt Quality

These leading questions complement the standard set of quality metrics. They spark a dialogue on whether the team *perceives* they are set up to meet product quality and delivery goals. Even more important perhaps than getting the right answers is simply enabling an open dialogue with the grassroots engineering team on the state of the product and the team mindset. The team is encouraged to go beyond just meeting the letter of the product quality... have they met the *spirit* of the product quality?

This opens communication channels in the team and allows for a broader set of factors to be considered when making business decisions.

For example, if many of the engineers are worried that the wrong measurements are being used to gage quality and that the true quality of the product is far worse than it seems, then this could spark a discussion and a change in operations. This is illustrated in the story below.

TEC Tames Quality by Numbers

Ron was working as a TEC with Jane's engineering team, monitoring the progress of the latest release. The team was working on a maintenance release, and the goal was to bring down the bug backlog as much as possible. By all accounts, the team was doing well: the bug backlogs were on track as per plan and each of the program reviews went smoothly. The release looked like it was going to be a success – at least on the surface.

The problem was that Ron knew Jane's engineers were really unhappy with her management of the release. Several of them had raised concerns that the metrics presented at the program meeting were all "smoke and mirrors". They were really not very confident about the release.

Jane took a singular focus on the bug reduction goal but lost sight of the bigger picture. This is what happened.

Each week Jane would put up a bug list in front of the engineers and list the number of bugs fixed by each engineer. This was supposed to motivate the engineers to fix more bugs per week and thereby increase software quality. Jane believed this added pressure helped drive the team to produce more results. She desperately wanted this release to succeed.

Ron, the TEC, saw things differently. He heard concerns about this practice from Jane's engineers. What actually ended up happening was that some engineers fixed bugs too quickly and caused more bugs to appear, which they subsequently fixed. Hence, the engineer that was most often at the top was also the engineer that introduced the most bugs into the product in the first place. The approach to quality was also disjoint. For the most part, each problem was point-fixed, which resulted in similar problems being fixed multiple of times, barnacled code, and increased costs arising from complexity and maintainability of code. However, what everyone saw was that Johnny fixed the most bugs and that a large number of bugs were fixed in the release – which gave a false confidence on the actual quality level of the product (as well as a false impression of Johnny's engineering abilities).

Jane's engineers were becoming increasingly unhappy with her management style and working on a product area that seemed to be spiraling downward. They were very much aware that the quality metrics used were shallow and did not measure the complexity of the changes or the real user impact.

Jane was in such a rush to get to the finish line and meet all her quality goals – that she lost sight of the team, their morale, and even the product quality. She was simply managing quality by numbers.

Ron also got feedback from the engineers about their perception of the product quality. This together with his hands-on evaluation and experience convinced him that Jane was going in the wrong direction. Not only was the product quality suffering, she was running the team ragged and seriously impacting their morale. There was a storm brewing and Ron knew he had to intervene.

Ron approached Jane and had an open discussion about the problems he was seeing. Jane was defensive, but Ron simply told her that he was there to help her. It was better for him to help Jane than for Jane to be found out at a later stage. Ron's only objective was to help Jane, the team and the product succeed. After some heated discussion, Jane saw the value in that. After all, Ron's job was to help in such situations and provide coaching. They discussed the problem in detail and brainstormed options.

The crux of the matter was that Jane absolutely had to bring down the backlog by a certain amount, and she counted on Johnny to make that happen. Ron suggested that she partner Johnny with another experienced engineer, Sue. Sue was known to be methodical and diligent in her work. She was also the one who was most vocal about the product quality. If Johnny can bundle all his changes together once a week, and have Sue review them to her high standards that might curtail many of the side-effects of Johnny's work. Jane saw the value in this but Sue and Johnny were polar opposites. Getting them to work together would be impossible. If they were able to, it would definitely make a world of difference to their product. Jane would have a good balance of speed and quality.

Ron and Jane each spoke with Sue and Johnny and coached them to work together. They provided ongoing *guidance and Ron even facilitated the initial discussions to get the ball rolling.*

The results were good. Although Jane still discussed the bugs fixed each week, she also discussed the complexity, and impact of the changes. She also solicited input from the broader team on any concerns regarding the changes. This open discussion was exactly what was needed to focus the team on building a quality product – and not just manage quality by numbers alone. The team could see that Jane did in fact care about the product quality – beyond just the metrics. Some of the changes were rejected based on this debate, and Johnny did not always make it to the top. However, the team as a whole was able to address the core quality issues, and believed that their approach would make a positive difference. Over the next month, the quality mindset started weaving itself into the team fabric.

This is an example of how the TEC's participation in the engineering team facilitated greater insight into simmering product quality issues – beyond raw numbers. The TEC's relationship with the engineering team is critical in getting direct feedback on how they perceived the true state of affairs. Ron could sense that they were becoming cynical about quality goals and was tuned into their dissatisfaction with the product. The TEC's impartiality also meant that he could provide guidance to the team and to Jane without being threatening. He has no skin in the game – other than to make the team successful. This made a huge difference in easing Jane's defensiveness, and made it easier to shape her behavior. As a result, the TEC was able to instill a more positive and sustainable quality mindset. This shift in mindset will have an impact on not just the current release – but on all subsequent releases. This is a lasting change, with sustainable impact to business results.

TEC - TRANSFORMS DAVID'S ADVENTURE

We opened the book with David's software adventure. It had all the hallmarks of a project that was bound to fail:

- a weak manager
- a difficult group of engineers
- unfinished tech transfer
- challenging deadlines
- lack of sponsorship
- Impossible and ambiguous product content

No wonder it failed!

How would a TEC have helped in this situation, and what impact would it have on the team, the product and overall success?

The following illustrates some of the ways in which a TEC could transform David's adventure.

- Hire the Right Manager

  The TEC could advise against hiring David. A project of such a magnitude and complexity requires an experienced manager. Although David wants to be a manager, this particular assignment is wrong. The project is too complex, and the engineers are too difficult for a first time manager. The TEC would work with the management team to find a suitable lead. In the meantime, the TEC would also work with David to help groom him for a more suitable management role.

- Provide coaching to the Prima Donnas

  There were a number of challenges within the engineering team. There were three prima donnas, each prone to over-engineering solutions and emotional dramas. Their skills were much needed. The TEC would work with these three engineers to build trust, and teamwork. This would make it more probable that these hot shots would to behave and perform effectively on the job. Taking this burden off the manager would allow the manager to focus on building the product roadmap and accelerating the deliverables.

- Coach the Management team to bond and build sponsorship

  The executives were not prepared to sponsor David and his team. They were unwilling to listen to his challenges and were dismissive of his concerns. This alienated David and his team, and the executives were blind to the real problems on the ground. Creating a bond between the engineering manager and the executive team is critical for product success. The TEC can facilitate this bond by coaching David to spend time building relationships with the executives. The TEC will also meet with the executives to solicit their sponsorship of David – and point out how critical that is for the team and project success. This "matchmaker" role for the TEC helps the management team gel together as a unit: it enables them to battle together rather than battling each other.

- Channel Communications across the team

  David faced formidable challenges in delivering his product. Certainly, gaining executive sponsorship would have helped him in garnering more help – such as adding more capable engineers to his team, extending timelines or reducing content. However, it is often difficult for executives to discern the truth from fluff: they are removed from the reality of what happens at the grassroots. Having an inexperienced manager whining about wanting more help is not something they may readily believe. This is another role for the TEC, who is an impartial and experienced third-party participant in the team. The TEC could vouch for what is real and what is fluff. This provides the executives with another data point against which they could base their decisions.

If a TEC were on board at the time of David's adventure, how will it play out? The following story illustrates a possible outcome.

David's Adventure – Replayed

The executive team has made a decision to invest in building Product Z. They were forming a new team and were looking for a manager.

Ron, the TEC, had been with the team for a month and had been well aware of this upcoming event. In fact, the executives had brought him into the team with this in mind. He had been using the time to build relationships with the team, and understand how things worked in the organization. Ron had been briefed about the criticality and complexity of Product Z, and knew that an experienced manager was a must.

David was well known to Ron. As soon as the management position was posted, David made his intentions known: he wanted that role. Product Z was cool, and David knew he had the technical skills to pull it off. The executives were thrilled that David was interested – he was one of their brightest engineers.

Ron however advised against David. Ron did not feel he had the maturity, operational savvy or people management skills to embark on such a complex project. However, he really thought David had good potential – just not as a manager on Product Z. Ron held discussions with the executives to share his views and encouraged them to create a growth plan for David. They could not afford to lose him. Part of the growth plan would be for David to take a leadership role in Product Z, managing some aspects of the project and delivery. Ron would coach him. Ron also held discussions with David and built up his enthusiasm for the new opportunity. He wanted David to feel good and have him buy into his new role – even though it was not the management position.

Ron worked with the executive team to find a suitable manager. They hired Rose, who had a strong track record for building solid engineering teams and delivering complex projects. Rose made it clear up front that she would need executive support to make the project successful. There can be no miracles. She was willing to work hard and make the team do the same. Rose also asked that Ron stay on board for four more months to help with the transition and facilitate a communications channel to the executives.

Ron partnered with Rose to put the team in order. He coached David, tamed the Prima Donnas and provided guidance on accelerating the tech transfer. Each of these was a "mini project" on its own, with many dramas to navigate. The toughest was the tech transfer. Ron managed this by requesting extra funds for the transfer to proceed smoothly. He earmarked a small bonus at each milestone and this gave added incentive to everyone. In addition, he asked one of the overseas lead engineers to come to North America for four months to become an expert in the technology. This freed up the team from having late night and early morning calls. Morale rose, and the transfer was accelerated.

Rose could focus on building a product roadmap and spend time building relationships with her team, her peers and her executives. With Ron's help, Rose was able to effectively communicate the challenges of her new team and charter to her executive management. Ron vouched for her. As a result, she was able to negotiate a revised *timeline and content for Product Z. This took several months to achieve – but, it made all the difference.*

Rose was able to successfully deliver Product Z with 75% of the requested content in about a year's time. More importantly, the team stayed intact and was highly energized. The initial investment in training the team on the new technology was worth it. The success spread: the customers put in new orders. As a result, a second team was started, and David became the manager. He had been grooming for this for one year, and now he was respected by his team and ready to take the reins.

The executives were proud of their achievements. They delivered an innovative product that was received well by customers. More importantly, they had unleashed the creative spirit in the team. Now, they can tackle a variety of engineering challenges. They felt invincible.

Success is possible, even in very challenging situations – if the right people-focused operations framework is put in place and the human elements within an organization are harnessed for maximum potential. A TEC is the catalyst for paving the way.

Summary: TEC Keeps the Spirit Alive

The problem of poor people management in engineering is widespread in the culture. People put up with it, but it impacts team effectiveness and productivity. Changing the habits of engineering managers and teams will take time. And that leaves the most important resource at hand – the engineering staff – in peril. Having an impartial and experienced team effectiveness coach – the TEC - can accelerate the change to people-focused operations. Key decisions will be made with more awareness: organizational structure, leadership, energizing the teams, recognition and rewards – and even project planning and delivery.

The role of the TEC is that of team counselor and cultural dynamics specialist. The coach is immersed into the very fabric of the engineering team. Through regular organizational diagnostics, the TEC is able to gather the pulse of the team on issues a variety of people issues. The perceptions and opinions of the team are then folded into the decision making process and thereby facilitate greater business success.

The TEC is the catalyst for creating and maintaining a positive, energized atmosphere that taps into the soul of software teams to maximize the full potential of the organization.

ORGANIZATIONAL DNA

When it comes to culture, walking the talk is important. Especially in the world of software engineering, where chaos and rush are staples of the environment, it is easy to lose track of these values altogether. There is *so* much focus on technology, and delivery. Everything is boiled down to metrics and answers are sought in binary formats. We sometimes simply forget to look at the nuances of human behavior to see if all parts of the organizational DNA are working effectively. How people work together, within the operational framework makes all the difference in creating a sustainable, profitable product.

People-focused operations involve tapping into the core areas of engineering culture and weaving these into the team operations. This starts with how to set up the organization, hiring practices, and how decisions are made about what to build, gauging quality, and managing transitions. Most software engineering teams have highly skilled and very logical individuals. They are not $10 an hour workers who can just be told what to do. They have to *believe* in what they do.

A team effectiveness coach – the TEC - is the lightning rod to spark discussions about organizational effectiveness, identify people issues and address them via team operations. Practicing these values within the operational framework strengthens the culture, and unleashes the spirit of software teams. This ultimately leads to stronger, happier teams which are more productive, innovative and drive product success.

Here is a summary of the success factors checklist that you can use for creating the people focused operations framework in your organization:

Organizational Success Factors	Your Organization
Nurturing Leadership	
Close knit community	
Software Soul	
People focused operations	
Managers are fully engaged	
Mutual respect between mgr and team	
Solicits and acts on feedback	
Continuous Improvement on team pulse	
TEC role fulfilled	

Section 6

Transformations

An Enlightened Path

To be is to do.... Immanuel Kant

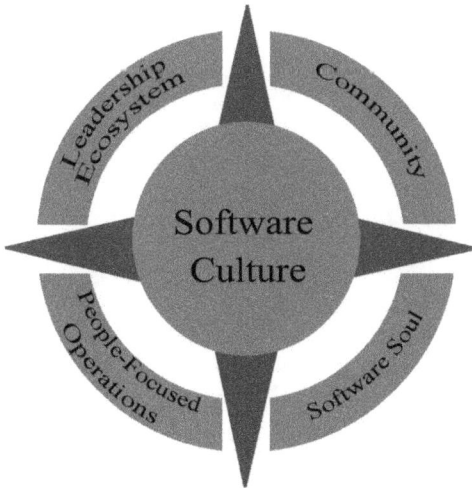

TRANSCENDING THE PRODUCT LIFECYCLE

The software product lifecycle provides a framework in which software is developed, tested and released. There are numerous milestones, metrics and processes to follow to ensure software products are reliably and predictably developed and released. Many new processes, tools and methodologies have been introduced to improve the chances of success. They have all helped to *some* extent. However, we still see teams of very smart software engineers, armed with these latest tools and techniques, that are struggling to succeed. It is time for a paradigm shift. There is a need to *transcend* the software product lifecycle – to encompass more than metrics and milestones - to fully harness the power of engineering teams.

This paradigm shift is achieved by refocusing on an engineering team's most important asset – its people.

There is a need for ongoing monitoring of the team pulse, raising awareness of gaps between espoused and practiced values and promoting good behaviors. Ultimately these behavior changes need to be woven into the very fabric of the organizational DNA. That is the foundation for a strong culture – which can be truly inspirational, and motivate teams to excel. Engineering teams that are driven by an internal compass strive do the right thing with minimal external guidance. They achieve the *spirit* as well as the *letter* of the product and company needs; they work beyond just metrics and milestones.

A strong engineering manager needs to be skillful at managing technology, operations and people. The fast paced environment and the singular focus on product delivery often times cause managers to sacrifice people issues in favor of getting things done. A typical engineering organization has specialists in the areas of program management and technology leadership. The idea of a Team Effectiveness Coach was introduced to complete the Engineering Triumvirate. Engineering leaders need assistance on managing their most important asset – their people. This is important especially in times of change or organizational flux. A TEC partners with the engineering manager to maximize team effectiveness. The TEC guides the engineering team to practice good behaviors as part of its operational framework. This impacts everything from hiring leaders, setting up the organization, inspiring the team, weaving meaningful measurements into product milestones and driving cultural changes.

Harnessing the full energy of engineering teams makes good business sense. Teams of effective engineers produce better software products – and fuel profitability.

It starts at the Roots of the Tree

I stated in the preface of this book that managing engineers did not come naturally to me – even though I consider myself a "people person". By and large, software engineers are an elite group of highly educated, talented individuals – most with high egos. Building an effective team out of these individual heroes, mentoring the team and driving it for success is truly an art.

Formal engineering management training tends to focus on handling logistics and project management mechanics. These techniques are certainly useful, but *completely insufficient* in managing people and setting up great teams. There is a need to refocus on management basics with an emphasis on the unique nature of software engineering: managing highly talented engineers, managing a diverse virtual workforce, promoting innovation, dealing with ambiguity, inspiring technical excellence, etc. This basic management training can't be done generically. It must be done in the context of software engineering - a unique culture that requires specialized people skills. There is a need to offer Team Effectiveness Coaching skills to all engineering people managers to enhance the business impact.

Another area for re-evaluation is how colleges train software engineers. I have hired many new grads, and most of them lack understanding of what it takes to actually design a product or be part of an engineering team. Most of the grads come from an environment where there is a "hero geek mentality" – the lone wolf that gets the A on the exam. While this type of training sharpens the technical and analytical abilities of the individual engineer, and makes them highly competitive, it does little to help new grads fit into the cultural ecosystem of software engineering. As a result, we see that many engineers are excellent at working by themselves with bounded problems, but struggle in teams or with ambiguity. When these engineers move into management, they propagate the hero geek mentality, and struggle with ambiguous decision making. This in turn impacts the effectiveness of engineering teams to work collaboratively or venture into new high risk, innovative areas. The complexity of today's software systems demands adaptability, creativity and ability to communicate effectively to solve problems. The need to collaborate and think creatively to solve engineering problems is critical to the success of software companies. The values engineers grow up with in school are the ones that are nearest and dearest to them. Change starts at the roots of the tree.

Colleges have an important role to play in seeding the next generation of software engineers. I strongly encourage colleges to re-evaluate their curriculums and emphasize "Real World Engineering". The training should include speakers who have worked as software engineers, software managers, and other software practitioners that can recount stories of what it takes to be effective and succeed in the engineering world. Stronger emphasis on teamwork, versatility, creativity, working in diverse virtual teams, and excellent communications are some of the critical skills that are needed.

Scientific leadership in the world is crucial for economic and social progress. This broad-based training of engineers and grounding them in the reality of how to succeed in the software industry can make a significant difference. Companies will benefit from new grads that can adapt more easily into the software engineering culture. The next generation of software engineering managers will learn from the roots of their education that working in the software industry requires more than just raw technical skills. A more rounded, innovative and balanced set of new grads will certainly make it easier for companies to integrate the individuals into their culture and grow the next generation of leaders.

At a personal level, my son is studying computer engineering and while I value his technical training and see that as being absolutely critical, I would certainly like him to have this broad education that includes the values discussed in this book. I believe it will make all the difference.

A Way Forward

As discussed earlier, the productivity of an engineering team can be significantly improved by creating a strong, vibrant culture where engineers and teams can work effectively together.

Overall costs can be reduced if there is a focus on organizational success – in addition to product success. This leads to greater productivity and ultimately to greater profitability for the company.

Harnessing the full potential of engineering teams, and maximizing organizational success requires weaving critical elements into the software culture:

- **Leadership Ecosystem**
  - Setting up a strong leadership framework
- **The Community**
  - Building Strong, Fun teams
- **The Software Soul**
  - Energizing, Inspiring atmosphere
- **People-Focused Operations**
  - Infusing people focus into team operations

The secret sauce is tapping into the *software soul* of the engineering team and unleashing their full potential within the operational framework of the product lifecycle. A major cultural change is required to make this happen. The change starts with a realization that the people in the organization can accomplish a lot more. A deeper change needs to start within the education system itself: how colleges train software engineers makes a world of difference in their ability to fit into the software culture.

It is up to *you* to realize the hidden potential and unleash the magic that is buried within your software engineering teams. We make choices each day – do you retain status quo or make changes to improve your culture? It is time to get off the treadmill and try a fresh approach to managing your software teams. Some of the ideas presented in this book are unorthodox. They are meant to spark a re-evaluation of what it takes to build great engineering teams and fuel productivity. You have the best understanding of your team and you know what may or may not work. There is no substitute being fully engaged in the engineering management process. Management by presence and full engagement with the engineering team and the leadership ecosystem will make a world of difference.

Go on, unleash the software soul, take the enlightened path and transform your organization into a truly magical and invincible team.

You will have a happier organization and your business will benefit greatly!

ABOUT THE AUTHOR

Mala Devlin has over 20 years in software engineering in a variety of technology firms. She has held positions such as software development engineer, and product manager before moving into engineering management. Mala has been a software engineering manager for 12 years and has driven many large, complex and cross functional projects to successful completion. She enjoys building strong teams and setting them up for success.

Mala was born in India, and moved to Montreal, Canada as a child. She grew up in a diverse neighborhood, attending school with immigrant children from different cultural and economic backgrounds. This experience has shaped her outlook and is why she values diversity as a key enabler for creativity and innovation. Mala has a Bachelors degree in Computer Engineering from McGill University.

Mala has been married for 20 years and is the mother of three teenagers. She attributes the challenges of motherhood in helping her to become more creative, patient and being able to think on the spot. In her spare time, Mala enjoys a variety of outdoor activities, including skiing, hiking and biking.

To learn more about The Software Soul and to join the discussion, visit www.TheSoftwareSoul.com

APPENDIX A: ORGANIZATIONAL SUCCESS FACTORS TEMPLATE

Organizational Success Factors	Your Organization
Nurturing Leadership	
- Engineering manager	
- Technical competence	
- Focus & Drive	
- Gain team mindshare	
- Active engagement with team	
- Performance management	
- People focus	
- Communication skills	
- Operational skills	
- Leadership ecosystem	
- Sponsor engineering manager	
- Foster collaborative peer Networks	
- Minimize bureaucracy	
Close knit community	
- Roles and Responsibility	
- Clarity and definition	
- Mutually agreed upon	
- Valued	
- Communications	
- % discussions in person vs virtual	
- Open & respectful discussions	
- Trusted communications	
- Geography	
Single site	
- > 75% project team collocation	
- ease of reconfiguring workspaces	
Multi site	
- Motivation: Cost vs. strategic	
- Self contained & fully owned charter	
- Tech transfer vs. new charter	
- Clear success criteria	
- Reporting to executive level	
- Continuous improvement process	
- International leadership exchange	

- Productivity of main-site team	
- Diversity	
- Gender	
% women & % men in staff	
% women & % men in leadership	
- Ethnic	
% women & % men in staff	
% women & % men in leadership	
- Skills	
Average number of years in team	
Exposure to other companies/orgs	
Exposure to other technologies	
- Team Esteem	
- How team sees itself	
- How others see the team	
- Team Rituals	
- Simple, regular, social gatherings	
- Casual, social connections	
- Team bonds	
Internal Compass	
Passion: driven to do right thing	
Pride of craftsmanship	
Engineering Values	
- Critical thinking	
- Innovation and Risk taking	
- Results over perception	
Rewards and Recognition	
- Incremental feedback	
- Peer input	
- Manage 'labels'	
- De-emphasize annual reviews	
Fair Promotions	
People focused operations	
Managers are fully engaged	
Mutual respect between mgr and team	
Solicits and acts on feedback	
Continuous Improvement for team pulse	
TEC role fulfilled	

APPENDIX B: WORDS AND PHRASES TO PONDER

In the course of writing this book, there were many thought provoking, and often funny terms people used to describe a situation. Before too long, I found myself using these terms in conversations with others. Many of these terms are already part of the engineering vocabulary, and some are new – but, they are all worthy of 'buzz' and hence warranted special mention. This is a collection of some of the more interesting terms.

Collaboration Cachet

> This term refers to the recent trend to have collaborative teams and the special cachet associated with participating on collaborative forums. Of course, everyone wants to be collaborative and it has huge business benefits – when implemented properly. Collaborative frameworks are more likely to succeed when there is mutual respect, shared values, common goals, and clear roles and responsibilities.

Cultural Atom

> The 'cultural atom' is nucleus of the engineering organization - the engineering manager. The engineering manager has the power to shape culture through their direct access to engineers. This in turn positions him to unleash tremendous energy at the grassroots level of the organization.

Cultural Dynamics Specialist

One of the interviewees jokingly called out the need for a 'cultural dynamics specialist' to oversee the organizational culture and ensure it stays healthy. This concept was eventually folded into the idea of a 'Team Effectiveness Coach'.

Diversity Inertia

'Diversity inertia' is the tendency of an organization to resist change – whether that change is to new ideas, new people or new ways of doing things. The inertia arises because people continue to do what comes naturally – and that is to retain the current operating mode.

Engineering Triumvirate

The leaders for the set of three focus areas in an engineering organization: technology, operations and people. The engineering manager retains full ownership for these critical areas in their organization – and indeed could very well play the role of leading all three areas. The triumvirate concept is that there may be times when advisors and specialists are needed to attain maximum success – hence, the need for a program manager, technical advisor and a team effectiveness coach.

Enronizing Metrics

This refers to the practice of manipulating software metrics to make the 'books look good'. Several of our interviewees recounted stories where the team was so focused on the 'metrics' required to ship the product that shortcuts were taken to make the numbers look good.

Harderware

One of our interviewees suggested that the term 'software' is a misnomer. It conveys the sense that the work is soft, easy and not serious. He suggested it should have been named 'harderware'. Perhaps, that would better describe the real nature of the challenges?

Leadership Density

The leadership density is the ratio of managers to engineers within a project or organization. An ideal scenario is to have the *minimum* number of people to make the project successful – and then to further optimize the number of managers that are really needed. Large projects that mushroom to tens or hundreds of engineers have the overhead of communications and coordination. A smaller team, with minimal management overhead, is more nimble and is more likely to make timely business decisions.

Leadership Ecosystem

This is the circle of leaders that make up the entire organization. A healthy thriving ecosystem is one where there is a nurturing, and supportive culture.

Legend in his own Mind

These 'legends' have simply nominated *themselves* into the category of greatness. You can easily spot them. They are the ones that love to talk about themselves, how important they are to the group, and offer advice about what needs to be done – even though they are very likely not willing to do the work themselves. This is a variation of the 'pontificating prima donna'.

Methodology Mania

The 'mania' is what happens when process, metrics and bureaucracy get in the way of doing the right thing. While methodology is good, and metrics are necessary – these are by no means sufficient to make business calls. The responsibility to deliver good software goes beyond metrics: judgment and qualitative assessments are also needed to make sound decisions.

Organizational DNA

The 'organizational DNA' is the unseen force that gives life to the entire organization. It is largely shaped by the organizational setup, and the culture. The DNA determines how the team operates, its values and ultimately its health and sustained success.

Organizational Heartbeat

This term is the same as 'Team Pulse' and is used to describe the general mood and cadence of the team. A healthy heartbeat exhibits itself in a committed team that is fully engaged in team goals and activities.

Pontificating Prima Donnas

The 'Pontificating Prima Donnas' are those that pontificate about solutions – but, never actually do the work to realize those solutions. You can spot them. They are the ones that talk incessantly, and sound great. In reality, they do very little work and rarely deliver on their promises.

PowerPoint Engineering

This is the concept that slick PowerPoint slides, depicting product concepts, are used as the medium of choice for 'engineering infomercials'. The lines become blurred between what is real and what is fantasy. What is easy to depict in PowerPoint, with linear roadmaps – often requires many iterations of engineering, fraught with failures to achieve final success. Even then, the final product may very well be different from the original vision. The spell of PowerPoint is powerful. It should be used as a springboard for in-depth technical discussions – and not as a means to decide what is and is not feasible in a product.

Programmer-Bot

The programmer-bot is the individual who simply codes and carries out the basic engineering tasks without questioning or debating. Very few engineers aspire to be 'programmer-bots'. However, some are forced into it when the culture inhibits open communications or is overly hierarchical.

Socio-Organizational

The socio-organizational fabric is the web of relationships and social norms that define an organization.

Software Imperialism

Offshore multi-site setups have proliferated in the last decade. Software imperialism is a concept that was presented to us by many grassroots managers and engineers, where they believe one of the key motivations for offshoring must be driven by a quest for power at the executive ranks.

Software Soul

The software soul is the very heart of what makes an engineer 'tick'. To bring out the best in an engineer, it is essential to unleash the spirit within the soul and let the energy drive success. You can certainly achieve pointed, short term wins without tapping into the soul – but, meaningful sustained results are possible only when the hearts of engineers are fully engaged.

Software Village

The software village is the ecosystem in which the engineering team lives. Indeed it takes the entire village to raise the engineer, the team and the project. A community spirit and a cooperative infrastructure are critical to sustained success.

Team Esteem

Team esteem is the collective esteem of the entire team. It is how much respect is bestowed on the team by the organization. Typically, it is a catch-22 in that 'type A' teams with high esteem attract top notch engineers and 'type B' teams with low esteem have the 'castaways'. An organization that wants strong players across the board needs to start by enabling strong team esteem.

Team Pulse

This term is used to describe the general mood and cadence of the team. A healthy pulse exhibits itself in a committed team that is fully engaged in team goals and activities.

Technical Virility

This term is quite often used to describe someone who has high technical vigor. We have heard it being used in the following way 'My manager thinks his technical virility is in question because we don't agree with him on all his technical decisions – and this makes him very insecure'.

Techno Babble

This is the stream of never ending technological terms and acronyms that inundate us every day and blur the focus on the real meaning behind the terms. We are told that techno babble is quite often used to 'spoof' and sell ideas as well as give the impression of knowledge 'by appearing geeky'. Many stated that techno babble puts them on guard and their 'spidey senses' go up: the motto being 'more lingo means less substance'.

Techno Fashionista

A techno fashionista is someone who is keenly aware and dedicated to garnering the latest technical gadgets. These are the folks that have the latest cell phones, know the latest techno trends and are in the forefront of defining 'cool geek'. They are extremely adept and leveraging technology to communicate in new and unique ways on the internet and through various devices. What is the downside of being a techno fashionista? This same group would quite often rather send email to their team mates as opposed to simply walking over and having a chat.

Vision Free

This term is used to describe a leader who is too carefree to create a vision. He has simply freed himself from the core management responsibilities and has achieved a state of being 'vision free'. This usually results in teams doing their own thing and not aligning with business priorities. We have heard the term used in the following way 'Joe is completely vision free. He is just too laid back to be bothered to create a vision for the team'.

Buzzwords that describe Management Styles

Bully Management

This is when management decides that the team will strive for a goal whether or not they believe in it. That is, they bully the team into submission. A classic example is when management sets an impossible date for an impossible milestone and uses high pressure tactics, such as 'you will lose your jobs' or 'we will cancel this project' to drive the team into frenzied action. Bully power may work in short sprints, but fails to achieve longer term, sustained success. Team members typically leave citing burn out, lack of trust and respect. Projects often go into major hacking mode during the sprint, and then are left with a massive cleanup after the fact. This technique is a sure fire way to alienate the team's spirit.

Chameleon Management

This is a management technique wherein the manager is adaptive to the situation at hand. For example, a normally 'go get em' manager may decide to purposefully let some of his team slow roll a deliverable so that the team can spend more time learning a new technology. Managers who practice chameleon management are able to modulate themselves to get the best from their teams.

Cowboy Management

Cowboy managers are those that used to be cowboy engineers. Their most valued skills are riding fast, being reckless, and saving the day. Mostly, they rush into a situation, create a commotion, corral the troops into order and claim success. They treasure heroism over teamwork and getting the job done at all costs over fostering relationships.

Microwave Management

This is very similar to 'bully management'. One engineer we spoke with used this term to state that his managers microwaved the engineers until they got the desired results. The only problem is that the heat dissipates quickly in microwaved foods, and analogously the engineers very quickly disappeared when the projects were completed.

Certainly, this is not a desired technique for sustained productivity.

Ostrich Management

This management technique describes the case where managers feel helpless and simply abdicate their responsibility. A classic example is where critical decisions need to be made about regarding project priorities. In 'Ostrich Management', the manager avoids making the decision and instead decides to keep status quo: slow roll features in parallel. The manager did not want to be seen as 'the bad guy' and instead let the team do whatever they wanted. The entire project team failed since there were no successes at all. Managers are paid to make difficult business decisions, and abdicating that responsibility results in failed businesses.

Seagull Management

This is when one more managers decide that a project is in trouble and warrants their attention. Without asking for input, the flock swoops over the troubled project, makes a lot of noise, 'poops all over it' and leaves. This gives the impression of lots activity – but, in reality the project is left in a mess and the team needs to work extra hard to clean up and get the project back on track.

Volcano Management

This is a manager who is unpredictable in his behavior – but, is generally simmering and just not very happy. Every once in a while the manager might explode and cause massive damage to the community around him. This type of person should be approached with great caution.

REFERENCES

[1] Dan Galorath on Project Estimating:

http://www.galorath.com/wp/software-project-failure-costs-billions-better-estimation-planning-can-help.php.

This is a summary of reports from the following organizations:

- Standish Chaos report 2009
- Oxford University regarding IT project success (Saur & Cuthbertson, 2003)
- British Computer Society (Jaques, 2004)
- National Institute of Standards and Consultants
- Tata Consultancy 2007
- Communications of the ACM Nov 2007: Sauer, Gemino, Reich

[2] Success Through Failure: the Paradox of Design by Henry Petroski, 2008.

[3] The Five Dysfunctions of a Team: A Leadership Fable by Patrick Lencioni, 2002.

[4] The Business Case for Gender Diversity' by Caroline Simard Phd. of the Anita Borg institute, 2009.